CONTACTING THE
SPIRIT
WORLD

CONTACTING THE
SPIRIT
WORLD

*How to develop your psychic abilities
and stay in touch with loved ones*

Linda Williamson

PIATKUS

Visit the Piatkus website!

Piatkus publishes a wide range of bestselling fiction and non-fiction, including books on health, mind, body & spirit, sex, self-help, cookery, biography and the paranormal.

If you want to:
- read descriptions of our popular titles
- buy our books over the internet
- take advantage of our special offers
- enter our monthly competition
- learn more about your favourite Piatkus authors

VISIT OUR WEBSITE AT: www.piatkus.co.uk

Acknowledgements:
The author wishes to thank the following publishers for permission to quote from their books: Celestial Arts, California – Elisabeth Kübler-Ross, *On Life After Death;* Rider – Sylvan Muldoon and Hereward Carrington, *The Projection of the Astral Body;* Aquarian – D. Scott Rogo, *Life After Death.*

First published 1996
Judy Piatkus (Publishers) Ltd
5 Windmill Street, London W1T 2JA
www.piatkus.co.uk

Reprinted 1997
Reprinted 1998
Reprinted 1999 (three times)
Reprinted 2001
Reprinted 2002

The moral right of the author has been asserted

A catalogue record for this book is available
from the British Library
ISBN 0–7499–1596–X pbk

Edited by Carol Franklin
Designed by Sue Rydall
Illustrations by Zena Flax

Printed and bound in Great Britain
by Biddles Ltd, *www.biddles.co.uk*

CONTENTS

INTRODUCTION

It's a funny thing about death. We know we've got to face it some day but we behave as though it didn't exist. We push it to the back of our minds and try to pretend that it's something that only happens to other people, like falling victim to a serious illness or being involved in a car accident. But there comes a point in the lives of each one of us when we can't run away from it any longer, when we are confronted with the death of someone whom we love. At such times even the most hardened of sceptics wonders whether death is really the end or whether there is something beyond.

Usually the question remains unanswered. Of course there is a period of mourning, but in time the grief subsides. It may leave behind an emptiness that can never be filled, but gradually things get back to normal and life goes on. Some people are not prepared to leave it at that, however. They have an urgent need to find out what has happened to the one who has gone. Have they ceased to exist, like a light going out, or are they living on in another world? If so, what kind of world is it? Is it possible to get in touch with them? Often there is a feeling that the dead person is still around, but then the doubts creep in. Are they really there or is it just imagination?

I asked myself these questions when my father died. I was in my early twenties at the time. He had been suffering from cancer for some months and I was glad that he was at least out of his pain, but we had been very close and I missed him terribly. I well remember his funeral. It was a cold, bleak day. The small circle of mourners was gathered around the grave, shivering. As the coffin was solemnly lowered into the earth the priest intoned the familiar words 'dust to dust, ashes to ashes' with about as much emotion as if he had been reading the football results. I did, however, have a source of comfort that the rest of the family was not able to share. Since early childhood I had had an instinctive belief in life after death. It was something I seemed to know without ever having been taught. I had always been aware of spirit presences around me. At times this had been disturbing but now it was a blessing because I could feel my father standing there. Being a practical person I could imagine he would be thinking what a load of nonsense all this was. We were not burying him, just the outworn body. So why didn't we stop feeling miserable, and go home and have our tea? I never went back to the cemetery. For me there was no need. He wasn't there. Often I felt him with me in the house. Once I remember standing at the sink doing the washing up, a job he had always hated, and hearing his voice in my mind saying with his customary humour, 'Well at least I don't have to wash the dishes any more!'.

I tried to tell my family he was there, but my words were met with disbelief. 'You're imagining it', I was told. I didn't think I was, but I had to be sure. I was already interested in spiritualism but I decided that I would look into it more and learn all I could about it. It was this that eventually led me to become a medium.

In the work I do now I meet many people who have suffered a similar loss. Most of them have never been to a medium before. They come out of desperation, not really knowing what to expect but seeking some sort of reassurance that death is not the end. That reassurance is what I, like all mediums, try to provide. I do this by attuning my mind to the spirit people, and passing on as best I can their love and whatever messages they want to convey.

These messages may be trivial in themselves, but often they are just what the person consulting the medium, who is called 'the sitter', needs to hear. Those who come back from the spirit world don't preach about the mysteries of life and death. They talk about simple, everyday things, just as they would have done when on earth. After all, they are still the same people they were here. They haven't suddenly sprouted wings and halos!

But a sitting, even a good one where the medium comes up with information that they couldn't possibly have known, may not be enough to convince. 'I want so much to believe', one woman said to me in tears, having lost her husband shortly before she came to see me, 'but I just can't be sure.'

I replied to her, as I do to anyone in her dilemma, 'I can't conclusively prove to you that life goes on after death. I can only offer you whatever I am able to receive. It's up to you to prove it for yourself.'

'How can I do that?' she wanted to know. I told her to go and see other mediums as well, and weigh up whatever she received from them. Often conviction builds up gradually over a number of sittings, as what one medium gives will be confirmed by another. I also advised her to read books on life after death. It helps to learn about other people's experiences and to see just how strong the case for survival is, despite the scepticism that exists – mainly among those who have never studied the subject!

Then I gave her another piece of advice that in the end was probably more important. 'If you really want to be sure that the person you love has survived death and lives on then you should learn to make your own contact with the spirit world.'

This is the advice I give to anyone who has suffered a bereavement. Of course, not everybody can become a fully fledged medium; not everyone would want to. But we can all develop a degree of sensitivity to the spiritual dimension. Once you have made this contact for yourself, then even if you can't actually see or hear your spirit people you will know that they are around you and this inner conviction is worth more than any evidence a medium can give.

Not all the sitters who come to me have suffered a bereavement. Over the last few years I have found that an increasing number of people, especially young people, come because they already feel themselves to be in touch with the spirit world. This awareness is something natural and instinctive. They don't need proof that there is another life. They accept this as an established fact. What they are looking for is help to develop their abilities so that they can be used in a positive way.

So this book is written with all these people in mind; those who want to become mediums, those who have been bereaved and those who are just curious to find out about the mysterious world beyond the grave. I have divided the book into two parts. Part I looks at contact with the dead that arises spontaneously through dreams, visions, hearing voices and in numerous other ways. It tells the stories of ordinary people who – perhaps like you – never thought they were psychic and in many cases never believed in life after death, but were forced to change their minds because of what happened to them. For, in fact, it is often the dead that contact us.

In Part II I have explained how you can go about developing your own ability as a medium. I can't promise that you will be a brilliant success. Becoming a medium isn't like learning to ride a bicycle. It isn't possible to give you instructions in ten easy lessons. How far you get depends on your inborn ability and your determination to work at it. But I can at least point you in the right direction and, once you start, you may surprise yourself by what you can achieve.

However, before we begin, and for the benefit of those who are new to the subject, it might be as well to understand something of what happens when we die, and what sort of world our loved ones are communicating from. Forget all you were ever taught about angels and harps, and forget the idea of a heaven somewhere far off in the clouds. It's much more interesting than that – and it's a good deal closer than you might think!

PART I

Spontaneous Contact With The Spirit World

1

THE THIN VEIL

'How can we know what the next world is like?' people often ask. 'No one has ever come back to tell us.'

But that's where they're wrong. There has always been contact between this world and the next. From the beginning of recorded history there have been accounts of ghosts, apparitions and spiritual visitations, both angelic and demonic. The Bible is full of tales of the supernatural – angels appearing to people and prophets who spoke in trance. Jesus appeared to his followers after his death. The famous Witch of Endor was in fact a medium who was used by Saul to call up the prophet Samuel. For mediums, too, have always existed, though they were regarded, rather like witches, as strange creatures not to be meddled with – an attitude which, come to think of it, is not all that uncommon today!

Since the spiritualist movement began over a hundred years ago, innumerable descriptions of the spirit world have come to us through many different mediums. When these are compared we find they paint a remarkably consistent picture. But that's not all we have to go on. We have another source of information, from the near-death experience (NDE), the accounts of those who have been physically dead and have been brought back to life by doctors.

The NDE

No one today can fail to have heard of the NDE. The subject first captured the imagination of the public in 1970 when the American psychiatrist, Dr Raymond Moody, published his book *Life After Life*, describing cases of people who had returned from death with astonishing stories of their glimpses into the Beyond. Since then many researchers have followed in his footsteps. Between them they have amassed thousands of cases – and the accounts they have collected are radically changing the way people feel about death and dying.

The most important point made by all NDEers (to use an Americanism) is that dying is not something we should fear. However much we dread it the actual moment of death is easy and painless. You just float out of your physical body. NDEers speak of death as a release. Dr Moody in his book quotes the words of a woman who was resuscitated after a heart attack.

> I began to experience the most wonderful feelings. I couldn't feel a thing in the world except peace, comfort, ease – just quiet. I felt that all my troubles were gone and I thought to myself 'Well, I'm quiet and peaceful and I don't hurt at all.'

In a typical NDE, and the experience does vary from one individual to another, the release from the body is followed by the sensation of travelling at tremendous speed down a long, dark tunnel. After this the person finds themself hovering somewhere near the ceiling looking down at their own body and, in the case of a death in hospital, watching the efforts of doctors and nurses to resuscitate them. Understandably, this comes as something of a surprise. Some

NDEers are thrown into a state of shock and cannot comprehend what has happened to them. They try to attract the attention of the people around and can't work out why no one can see them. Others, however, suffer nothing of this confusion. For them the experience is a blissful one. They feel utterly contented and at peace, and watch the scene that is being enacted with detachment as though the physical body had no meaning for them any more.

But whatever their reaction to this sudden transition it is clear to them all that they are very much alive. They still have a body which looks like the body they have just left but which seems to be composed of a finer material. It is weightless and can move effortlessly through space, even, like the traditional ghost, passing through doors and walls. This new body does not suffer any of the pain or disabilities of the physical body. One woman who had been blind discovered to her joy that she could see.

Amid all these strange and bewildering events, it is comforting to know that all NDEers say they are met and helped. Generally, it is a close relative who comes to greet them, someone with whom they have a close bond of affection. In some cases it may be a 'guardian angel', a spirit who has been appointed to watch over them. Sometimes they are told by this person that they must return to their bodies as it is not yet time for them to die, whereupon they regain consciousness. But a few people are transported for a brief time beyond the boundary of death.

They are taken to a world of great beauty, which resembles the earth but in an idealised form. Numerous accounts speak of beautiful scenery, trees, birds, flowers and magnificent buildings. The light is dazzling but does not hurt the eyes. Often they are met by a Being of Light some describe as Jesus. Deceased friends and relatives are waiting for them. All is peace and harmony.

One of the most complete accounts of the near-death

experience is given by Betty Eadie in her book *Embraced by the Light*. Betty is an American housewife who died after an operation. It was some hours before the doctors were able to revive her, but when she regained consciousness she retained the memory of a profound and moving experience during the course of which she was taken by spirit helpers to a garden:

> As we went outdoors into the garden I saw mountains, spectacular valleys, and rivers in the distance. My escorts left me, and I was allowed to proceed alone, perhaps to experience the full beauty of the garden unencumbered by the presence of others. The garden was filled with trees and flowers and plants that somehow made their setting seem inevitable, as if they were meant to be exactly how and where they were. I walked on the grass for a time. It was crisp, cool, and brilliant green, and it felt alive under my feet. But what filled me with awe in the garden more than anything were the intense colours. We have nothing like them.

Spirit communicators describe their world in similar terms. In fact, it is amazing how NDEers, many of whom had no previous belief in life after death and had probably never read a book on the subject, echo so precisely what we are told from the other side of life.

Perhaps it is not surprising that those who are privileged to have these brief, tantalising glimpses of the beyond do not want to come back to earth. They all tell of their reluctance to return and of the unpleasant shock of waking up in their body. But they come back transformed by their experience. They have lost their fear of death and their whole outlook on life has changed. They are less interested in money and worldly success, and have an increased compassion for others and sense of purpose in life. While not necessarily becoming religious in any conventional sense, they often develop a deep spirituality, even if they were atheists before.

In some cases they have become psychic and exhibit mediumistic abilities. Dr Melvin Morse, an American paediatrician, who has researched the near-death experience for many years, has found that NDEers are four times more likely to have psychic experiences than those who have not had NDEs. He discovered that some of them retained contact with their 'guardian angels' or the spirit people they met long after they returned to life, and were able to call upon them in times of need. He believes that these things happen because the NDE activates the part of the brain that is responsible for paranormal powers.

Proof Of Life After Death?

But does the NDE really prove life after death? Many people believe it does. Some scientists have tried to explain it away as a hallucination. They claim that the dying brain is deprived of oxygen and this brings about a form of delirium called hypoxia in which vivid hallucinations can occur. NDEs have also been linked to a condition known as autoscopy, in which patients, usually those suffering from migraine, epilepsy or extreme stress, see a projected image of themselves, as NDEers report looking down on their own bodies from a vantage point several feet above.

These explanations, however, fail to give reasons for some very significant facts. The NDE is not like any hallucination known to science, whether induced by drugs, anaesthetic or any other cause. The experience is logical and coherent, and more vivid than any dream. There is a remarkable consistency in NDE accounts across a broad spectrum of people of all types and nationalities. It is hardly likely that they would share the same delusion. Nor can science account for the mental and spiritual transformation NDEers undergo. Far from being victims of a short-term derangement of the brain, they return to their bodies with a fundamentally changed outlook on life, like those who have undergone a profound religious experience.

NDEs do not only happen to those who expect life after death. Atheists are as likely to have them as believers. In fact, some religious believers have expressed surprise that what happened to them was very different from what their faith had led them to expect. We also have to take into account the evidence of those who, on returning to the body, have reported events or conversations which took place while they were clinically dead and which have been verified. Some NDEers have travelled in their disembodied state out of the room where their body was lying and were able to witness events taking place in nearby rooms or even at great distances away.

A Peep Behind Death's Curtain

So the NDE gives us a very reassuring idea of what it is like to die. But how accurate a picture does it give of the next world? I suspect that it is a very limited one, rather like the difference between going on a day trip to Calais and actually going to live in France. For NDEers only get a brief peep behind death's curtain. To find out more, we need to look at the information given to us by those who are living there.

The first thing to grasp about the spirit world is that it is not really a place. Traditionally, of course, we think of it as being in the sky or among the stars, but that is as mistaken as the idea of God as an old man sitting on a cloud, looking down on the earth from a great height. It would be more accurate to describe it as a different state of existence where time and space as we know them do not apply. And that, incidentally, answers another question that is frequently asked: 'How can there be room "up there" for all the millions of people who have died since the world began?' There are no limits to the spiritual dimension. Like eternity, it has no beginning and no end.

The Structure of the Spirit World

I have said that it is not a place and therefore it cannot be located in geographical space, but in order to give some idea of the structure of the spirit world I will use an analogy. Imagine a series of concentric circles, each one interpenetrating the other. Each circle is composed of finer material and vibrates at a higher frequency than the one before.

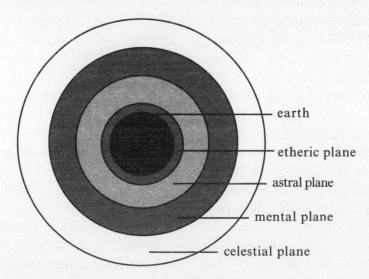

earth

etheric plane

astral plane

mental plane

celestial plane

The planes of existence

In the middle is the earth. This is the darkest, most dense of the worlds. Spirit communicators say that it is grey and heavy by comparison with the world they inhabit, and that for them to come down to this level is like a diver descending to the depths of the ocean. Immediately surrounding the earth (figuratively speaking) is the etheric plane. This is a dim, misty region that forms a borderland between the earth and the invisible spheres. Most souls, when they die, pass through this region quickly, like passing through a mist. Others remain here for a while, in a dreamlike state, until they are fully awakened to their new existence.

The Summerland

There are no hard and fast barriers between one dimension and the next, so the etheric dimension shades into the astral. This is the plane so vividly described in NDE accounts. It is where we normally go after death. In spiritualist literature it is called the Summerland.

In my book *Mediums and the Afterlife* I explain something of the nature of this mysterious realm. Basically, it is a plane of thought, created by beings on a higher dimension as a place where newly arrived souls can feel at home. It is not heaven though it may seem blissful and it's surprisingly like our world. There are no mechanical devices such as cars or telephones since these are not needed, but the inhabitants have spirit bodies which resemble earthly bodies, live in houses and do many of the things we do here.

Some souls spend only a short time in the Summerland, others may stay for centuries – time has no meaning there. But eventually there comes a point at which they move on. Then, they may return to the earth in a new body to gain fresh experiences and learn new lessons, or they may progress into higher dimensions.

The Higher Spheres

These higher dimensions which lie beyond the astral plane are so utterly unlike our world that it is hard to form any concept of what they are like. According to occult teaching, the next plane beyond the astral is the mental plane. The highest level of all is the celestial sphere, which is a state of God-consciousness that cannot be comprehended in earthly terms but which might be called heaven.

But the spirit people whom mediums contact are not speaking from these far-off regions. They are existing on the astral level. Although they are usually (though not invariably) wiser than we are, their knowledge is limited and they are not infallible sources of wisdom. Some communicators do come from dimensions beyond the astral, however, and these we call guides or teachers. In some traditions they might be thought of as angels. They have been in the spirit world longer and have progressed further, but even they have not reached the final heaven.

A Kind of Hell

What about hell, you may ask? I don't for a moment believe in the traditional hell of fire and brimstone with little demons in red suits sticking forks into people. But a kind of hell does exist. The NDE sheds light on this aspect of the Afterlife too. A tiny minority of people have what are called negative NDEs, in which they encounter demonic figures and nightmare images that fill them with terror. This doesn't mean that they are bad people. They have just been unfortunate enough to glimpse the hell regions of the astral plane, which, however, are more likely to be bleak and cold than hot and smoky.

After death we gravitate, by a natural law of attraction, to the plane for which we are most suited. They are all planes of thought, so in a sense we create our own heaven or hell, by our own thoughts and personalities while we are living this life. The majority of people have lived fairly decent lives and earned a rest, but anyone who had led an evil life, deliberately inflicting pain and suffering on others, would pay for it by being confined to this joyless region where they would have a tough time of it.

No one has ever come back and said that they were hauled up before the throne of God to be judged, but NDEers speak of a life review, during which the events of their lives flash before them like a video being replayed. They are obliged not only to acknowledge what they have done wrong but, what is worse, to feel within themselves the hurt they have inflicted on others. Although they are guided through this review with great love and understanding, it is nevertheless painful.

Spirit communicators also say that, at some time, they have had to review their earthly lives. They go through a period of remorse which may plunge the soul into a temporary hell of its own making, but even this is a self-judgement, not divine retribution. And what counts when you look back on your own life is not what you have believed, or whether or not you went to church, but what sort of person you were. In other words, plain, old-fashioned goodness and kind heartedness will get you further in the next world than any hymn singing and empty chanting of prayers.

This brief sketch I have drawn of the Afterworld is obviously very simplistic. There are numerous planes and conditions there, and all of them are different. It is not a case of being sent to one place for all eternity. Souls can move from one level to another. Even an evil person would eventually, after a period of remorse and atonement, be able to progress upwards towards the light.

Traesa's NDE

The NDE is not uncommon. During my years as a medium I have listened to many people telling how they died and came back to life again. A number of accounts were told to me while I was compiling this book. One of the most moving came from Traesa, an Irish woman who has lived in London for many years. Her story is unusual, in that she shared with her uncle his transition into the next world.

Traesa's uncle lived a hermit-like existence in a hut on a hill. As a child, she often used to visit him. One day when she went there he was very ill. As she said goodbye to him she added, as she always did, 'I'll see you again'. The old man propped himself up on his elbow and said very earnestly, 'Yes, you will see me again, Tossle' (his pet name for her).

> Shortly afterwards, I dreamed I was walking up the hill to the hut where he lived. He was walking beside me, but it was as if we were going through a tunnel into light. I said to him, 'Can I walk all the way with you?' But he said, 'No, you must go back now.' I didn't want to. The light was so beautiful and so loving, I didn't want it to end, but he insisted and I never argued with Uncle Jack. I turned back but he went on and zoomed into the light. Later, I discovered that he had died in hospital that night.

Traesa added, 'I know that, when my time comes, I will see that light and I won't be afraid.'

That, above all, is what the NDE teaches us; that death is nothing to fear. In her book *On Life After Death* the famous American psychiatrist Dr Elisabeth Kübler-Ross has this to say:

We have hundreds of cases, from Australia to California. They all share the same common denominator. They are all fully aware of shedding their physical body, and death, as we understand it in scientific language, does not really exist. Death is simply a shedding of the physical body like the butterfly shedding its cocoon. It is a transition to a higher state of consciousness where you continue to perceive, to understand, to laugh, and to be able to grow. The only thing you lose is something that you don't need anymore, your physical body. It's like putting away your winter coat when spring comes, you know that the coat is shabby and you don't want to wear it anymore. That's virtually what death is all about.

The veil between that after-death world and ours is a thin one. When we communicate with it, we are not talking to angels nor are we dealing with wraiths in misty shrouds. We are contacting ordinary people we have known and loved. And it is to the subject of communication that we will now turn.

2

MEDIUMS AND SITTERS

Some of the people who come to me for sittings, or readings as they are also called, are decidedly nervous. All they know about mediums has come from watching horror films or reading ghost stories and they have the strangest ideas about what is going to happen. I can recognise these nervous sitters. They enter the room timidly, looking around as if they expect ghosts to fly out from behind the curtain. Then they perch on the edge of their seats, waiting for me to put the lights out and go into trance.

I always reassure them that I have no intention of doing either of these things. They are relieved by this and to discover that I am comparatively normal. They are further relieved to see that my cat, who usually sits beside me (occupying my chair so that I have to sit on the settee) shows no sign of disturbance but snoozes quietly through the whole proceedings.

Actually, nothing spooky happens during a sitting. I do not expect my visitors to join hands round a table. I merely sit and talk to them. My function is to act as a messenger, attuning my mind to their loved ones in the spirit world and passing on as accurately as I can whatever the spirit people want to say. But I do understand my sitters' apprehension.

The whole subject of death and the afterlife provokes fear and unease – most of which is based on ignorance and superstition.

Common Superstitions About Mediums

One of the most common superstitions is that mediums call up the dead. Every medium gets tired of hearing this old cliché. The dead are more alive than we are, in the higher dimension in which they exist. We do not call them up. They come back because they want to, because of their love and concern for their family and friends on earth. No medium can make anyone return against their will. Some people choose not to come back at all, and personally I don't blame them!

Another mistaken belief is that mediumship is dangerous because it is 'dabbling in the occult'. This, too, is a tired old cliché that is trotted out again and again. By 'occult', people usually mean witchcraft and black magic. There is no connection between mediumship and witchcraft. We do not evoke dark forces. Come to that, neither do modern witches, who have also been given a bad press. This is not to deny that forces of darkness do exist. If you play around with voodoo or Satanism you are asking for trouble. But there is nothing sinister in the simple, natural contact with loving beings in the Beyond. There is a spiritual law that like attracts like. If you have evil in your heart you will attract evil, but if you send out love you will draw love and light around yourself.

The fear of possession also troubles some people. Cases of possession have been known but they are very rare. When you understand how difficult it is for those in spirit even to make us aware of their presence, you will see that for any spirit to take over someone in the body is almost an impossibility. It is possible, however, for a spirit being to impinge mentally upon someone on earth, and influence their thoughts and behaviour. This may happen with a person who is mentally weak or whose mind is damaged by mental illness. Some mental patients who claim to hear voices are suffering from this sort of intrusion. But no one in a normal state of mind can be taken over or possessed. You certainly cannot become possessed by your own spirit loved ones. Mediums do not become possessed, even when in trance. They are working in willing co-operation with spirit helpers.

Ouija Boards

I am often asked about the use of ouija boards to contact the spirit world. An ouija board, which takes its name from the French and German words for 'yes', is a smooth board with the letters of the alphabet printed round the edge. An upturned glass is placed in the centre. The operators each place a fingertip on the top of the glass and utter the time-honoured question, 'Is there anybody there?' The glass then moves, supposedly pushed by the spirits, and spells out messages. There is also a device called a planchette. This is a triangular-shaped pointer with a pencil at one end and two rollers which enable it to glide over paper. It works in a similar way. The participants place their fingertips on the pointer, which then, hopefully, writes messages on the paper.

If these devices are used by experienced mediums they can produce interesting results, but they are a slow and laborious means of communication. Imagine trying to hold a conversation with someone if you had to spell out every word! However, they are not toys and I would advise anyone who is inexperienced to leave them well alone. For one thing, they can be a great waste of time. Often all you get is a meaningless jumble of letters or illegible scribble. If you do get decipherable messages, it is impossible to tell how much is coming from spirit and how much is coming from your own mind. Even though you are not consciously pushing the glass or the pointer, you can do so without being aware of it and all you are communicating with is your own subconscious.

There is also a danger that you may attract the sort of spirits you would rather not have around you. Most of these will be harmless but there is also what you might call the yob element of the spirit world who like to spread fear and confusion whenever they get a chance. This is only a very slight danger since, as I have said, if you seek in love and sincerity you will attract nothing but good. But if you treat it as a game, and perhaps invite others to take part whose motives may not be as sincere as your own, then you are making it possible for such beings to slip in undetected. It is far better to make your contact through developing your spiritual awareness than to rely on mechanical devices.

Spiritualism

Spiritualism has an unfortunate reputation. It is associated with little old ladies holding seances in back parlours. Many people do not realise that it is a recognised religion, which began in America in 1848 with two sisters, Kate and Margaret Fox, whose home in Hydesville, New York State, was being plagued by a ghost. The sisters succeeded in communicating with the spirit, who told them he was a pedlar who had been murdered there and his body buried in the cellar. Years later, excavations uncovered human bones and a pedlar's tin. News of the happenings in Hydesville spread rapidly and led to a craze. All over America, people were trying to contact the spirits. They would sit around a table, while the spirits communicated by causing the table to move or making rapping noises.

Crude though these methods seem today, at the time it was a breakthrough. For the first time in history, ordinary men and women realised that it was possible to get in touch with those they knew who had died. No doubt there was a lot of self-deception. Tables, like glasses on ouija boards, can be moved by the unconscious action of the sitters. There was also a lot of fraud. But there was genuine phenomena too which gave verifiable evidence of life after death.

Spiritualism soon spread from America to England and other countries. Churches were formed and many people discovered that they had a gift for mediumship. In time, the style of mediumship changed. Rapping tables and dim seance rooms were replaced by mediums linking mentally with the spirit world.

Today, there are hundreds of spiritualist churches in the UK and all over the world. They offer services similar to those held in non-conformist churches, in that they are quite informal, and include hymns and prayers. Every service also includes a demonstration of mediumship, commonly called clairvoyance, at which the medium passes on short 'messages' from spirits to members of the congregation.

Sadly, the standard of mediumship in churches often leaves a lot to be desired and newcomers may go away completely unconvinced. But it is worth visiting a number of different churches and seeing a number of mediums in order to form a balanced view, since some of them are excellent.

Anyone can go to a spiritualist church service and there is no need to be nervous about doing so. They are not held in darkness and you will not see a trace of an apparition. The atmosphere is nearly always warm and welcoming.

Churches also offer other activities such as lectures, discussion groups and what are called development circles, which are for the training of mediums. Spiritual healing, too, is available. If you feel the need of healing, whether you are seriously ill or just a little under the weather, this is well worth trying as it can help on all levels, spiritual and emotional, as well as physical.

Not all mediums work within the spiritualist movement, though the majority do. They travel from church to church taking services and many also give private sittings in their own homes. My own work is divided between visiting churches and giving sittings. I also conduct seminars and workshops on the development of mediumship.

Beliefs of Spiritualism

The main tenet of spiritualism is that the soul survives physical death and lives on eternally. It offers proof of this through communication with the spirit world. Its philosophy about life and the hereafter is based on the received wisdom of many spirit teachers. It sees good in all religions, but believes that no one religion holds the whole truth. It constantly emphasises the importance of love and service as the basis of all religions. The purpose of life on earth is to learn and grow, so that we become more spiritual beings and express the spark of divinity that is within each one of us.

Spiritualism respects Jesus, as it respects all great spiritual teachers. There is a Christian spiritualist movement which looks to Jesus as the greatest master of all, although they would not necessarily go along with all the doctrines of the church. But spiritualism is regarded with suspicion by the Christian church, particularly by some Evangelicals and Fundamentalists who regard it as the work of the devil, and think all spirits who communicate with the earth are demons in disguise.

I find this kind of prejudice rather sad. In all the years I have worked as a medium, I have felt nothing but love from the spirit world. I have seen broken hearts mended and lives transformed by the knowledge that life goes on. And all I can say is if that is the work of the devil, then the devil must be not such a bad chap after all!

How Mediums Can Help

It is sometimes alleged that mediums make it harder for people to get over the loss of loved ones by encouraging them to cling to the person who has died. In my experience, this is not the case. Anyone who has lost someone they love will know the despair this brings. The worst part of it is feeling that they have simply ceased to exist and that you will never see them again. Mediums cannot, of course, take away the pain grief causes, but they can ease this pain by showing that the dead live on and that loved ones will one day be reunited. It is easier to overcome your grief if you know that they are well and happy.

Certainly, those in spirit don't want us to cling to sad memories. 'Don't sit there moping, go out and enjoy yourself!' is the sort of message I am often given to pass on.

The people who find it hardest to take this advice are the ones who are harbouring regrets. Perhaps they never had the chance to say goodbye to someone who died suddenly, or maybe they wish they had behaved differently when the person was on earth, or expressed their love more. Here, mediumship can have a healing quality. A sitting provides the opportunity for those on both sides of life to say what they need to say and to heal the wounds.

One woman's mother came to say, 'Tell my daughter to forget about that stupid argument we had. It was my fault. I want her to know I still love her.'

The woman's face lit up. 'I needed to hear that,' she said. And she told me that she and her mother, with whom she normally got on well, had had a tiff. She had been going to ring her up but, before she could do so, her mother had a stroke and died. Even since then, she had been worried that her mother had not forgiven her. Now she was able to put the guilt out of her mind and get on with her life with a clear conscience.

Sitters' Concerns

In the period following a person's death, those who have been close to them often feel their presence in the home. This is a very common occurance. In fact, I seldom have a sitter who has not felt this sense of presence. They naturally want to know whether it is just their imagination. I always assure them that what they feel is real and that their loved one is trying to reach them. Trust your own intuition – and don't be put off by those who say, or imply, that you have become temporarily unhinged and that you'll come to your senses when you get over it!

The sitter's first concern is to know that their friend or relative is alright. 'Is he at rest?' they ask. I dislike this expression. It recalls the ideas of the dead sleeping in their tombs until the Day of Judgement, which is very far from the truth. I prefer to think of the next world in terms of joyful activity. There is no sickness or disease there. These things belong to the physical body and are left behind when the spirit body is released. A person who had lost a limb would be complete in their spirit body. Disabilities like blindness and deafness also disappear. Often the first thing communicators say is, 'I've got my strength back' or 'I can walk again'. So I tell my sitters, when you remember them, don't think of them as they were old and sick. Think of them as being strong and healthy, because that's how they are now.

There is no hard and fast rule about how soon people can come back. I have known them to come back before their funerals and to be very interested in the arrangements being made for their send-off! A person who had died a violent death might find it hard to communicate clearly. People who are catapulted suddenly out of physical existence, perhaps as a result of an accident, may be in a state of shock, not knowing what has happened to them. How quickly they overcome this confusion depends on the individual, but help is always given in the spirit world and usually it isn't long before they accept their transition. I have had communication from many accident victims and they had all adjusted quite happily. In most cases they say they have learned that there was a reason for their sudden departure, and that what looked like an accident from an earthly point of view was actually part of a spiritual plan.

Suicides

People who take their own lives are often full of regret when they find themselves in the spirit world. Sometimes they, too, are confused. It is interesting that a significant number of those who have had negative NDEs had been attempting suicide. But all suicides are met with love and understanding, and they can and do communicate.

One of the most moving sittings I ever gave was for a woman whose teenage son had taken his own life. She was reproaching herself bitterly, thinking that it was in some way her fault and that she should have seen the danger signs. Her son told her that she was in no way to blame and that he had acted in a fit of depression, when he scarcely knew what he was doing. He said he was with his grandparents who were taking care of him. He wished he hadn't done it but he was slowly beginning to come to terms with the situation. Knowing this, his mother was able to accept what had happened and forgive herself.

Death and Children

The death of a child is always a terrible tragedy for the parents, who feel that their son or daughter has been denied the opportunity to grow up. But children grow up in the spirit world, looked after either by members of their families or by souls specially chosen to do this work. They remain closely in touch with their parents on earth, and develop into beautiful souls who can bring much comfort and enlightenment.

Animals

Animals, too, survive death. They have souls, just as surely as we do. There is a soul in every being that God has created. It is only humankind's conceit that makes us think that we alone should be specially endowed. Animals can come back to their owners. When I get 'up there' I fully expect to find beloved cats waiting for me, purring and demanding a lap to sit on!

Marriage

The question of marriage is one that often comes up. 'Are people always with their spouses in the next world?' is a common question. This is not inevitably so. If two people loved each other they would be together, but if there was no real affinity they would go their separate ways. Anxiety sometimes arises when a sitter whose partner has been dead for some time meets someone else and perhaps wants to get married again. 'Will he be jealous?' a widow wanted to know. I suppose it is possible, but I have never come across jealousy under these circumstances. 'All I want is for you to be happy', was the message from her husband. 'I'm glad you've found someone to take care of you.'

One elderly man came to me very concerned that his second wife, who had recently died, might have met his first wife who had died many years before. He needn't have worried. They came together and were apparently the best of friends.

But I had to laugh at the reaction of one sitter when I told her that her husband had met someone called Molly in the spirit world.

'Is he with that woman again?' she fumed. Molly was apparently an old flame. 'I'll kill him when I get up there!'

I am often asked whether anyone in spirit can be contacted. The question is often followed by a remark like, 'Only I haven't heard from Uncle Jim for a few years and I'd like to know why Aunt Ethel left me out of her will.'

I can't oblige with such requests. Not everyone is able to come back. Not everyone wants to. Some don't believe it is possible – there are as many unbelievers on the other side of life as there are on this. Those who come through in a sitting are generally, as you would expect, those closest to the sitter. It is the link of love that draws them. But nothing can be guaranteed. Sometimes people you hardly know come back, while your nearest and dearest fail to put in an appearance.

'Six months my husband's been gone,' one woman complained, 'and in all that time I haven't heard a peep out of him!'

Looking at her I wasn't surprised. She'd given him a hard time when he was here. I hope he had forgiven her – but I couldn't blame him for staying away.

The Communicators

I was surprised, when I first began to learn about contact with the next world, how very human the communicators are. They do not come back as great saints or philosophers. They are ordinary men and women, showing a natural concern for those they cared for on earth, talking about ordinary things. The criticism is often made of spiritualism that the messages are trivial – but everyday conversation between people on earth is trivial, or seems so to outsiders though, of course, to the persons concerned, it is very meaningful. This is why I always speak of 'spirit people', rather than calling them 'beings' or 'entities'. If, say, your mother comes back to talk to you, she is still your mother, not an 'entity' – and certainly not a ghost.

They appear as they did on earth. They even wear the same sort of clothes. This is not really so strange. When we are in the astral world we create our own clothing automatically, by the power of thought. If you want to create different garments for yourself you can, again by thought, but most people come back in their familiar clothes. Sometimes this is for the purposes of recognition. They wear (or give me a mental picture of themselves wearing) something the sitter would remember. One man appeared in overalls because that was how his daughter thought of him – wearing greasy overalls, tinkering about with the car!

Of course, they do change over a period of time, as they move forward on to higher dimensions. The astral plane is not a static state. If it were, there would be no progress. Someone who had been in the spirit world for many years would have changed. They would still be essentially the same person but they have grown in wisdom and their horizons would have been broadened. Spirit teachers

who have been in that dimension for many years communicate from a higher plane and do not concern themselves so much with the mundane details of people's lives,
but more with guiding their spiritual development.

There is one thing I find frustrating about my work as a
medium, and that is the limitations of communication. I am
constantly aware that the spirit people want to say far more
to the sitters than my mind is able to receive. I do not physically hear or see them. The communication takes place on a
mental level. (This does away with the language problem – I
receive the thoughts, rather than the words, so it does not
matter if the communicator does not speak my language.)
For them, it is rather like trying to speak on a faint tele-
phone line, with a lot of crackling and interference. They
would dearly love to sit down and have a good chat with the
person they want to contact, but all they can manage is a
few, possibly disjointed, words and short messages.

But communication works on the power of love. Where
there is love and sincerity, the contact can be made and the
closeness of the spirit world can be experienced by anyone
who is prepared to open their hearts and minds – as I will be
making clear later in this book.

3

ASTRAL JOURNEYS

We may intuitively know that the invisible part of our being that lives beyond death, the soul, spirit, call it what you will, exists, but it can't be proved – or can it?

The word 'soul' is one that most scientists are uncomfortable with. It does not fit in neatly with their mechanical theories about the universe. But there is a growing body of scientific evidence to indicate that there is something in people that can exist independently of the physical body. This evidence comes from studies of out-of-the-body experiences, or OOBEs.

Studies Of OOBEs

The OOBE is very common. There are numerous accounts of people leaving their physical bodies, usually though not always in sleep and floating around in a disembodied state. A number of psychics claim to be able to do this at will and their claims have been tested in the laboratory. Of these, one of the most famous was Alex Tanous.

Tanous, an American college tutor, was put through a series of tests by the parapsychologist, Karlis Osis. Tanous was put in a sound-proofed cubicle and asked to project himself out of the body, travel to a distant room and describe some pictures that had been placed there. He achieved a 65 per cent success rate in describing the pictures correctly. Further experiments were devised to see if he could affect physical objects while out of the body. In one experiment, sensitive instruments called thermistors which register any slight change in temperature were placed in another room. Tanous, projecting himself from his cubicle, was able to trigger them off. Another experiment used light-sensing devices which were set up in a darkroom in another part of the building. When he claimed to be projecting, the instruments registered a sudden and otherwise inexplicable increase in light.

Dr Charles Tart, a pioneer in the field of altered states of consciousness, has also carried out extensive research into OOBEs. One of his subjects, 'Miss Z', a woman in her early twenties who claimed to have had OOBEs since she was a child, was invited to take part. Tart built a shelf near the ceiling of the room in the laboratory where she was sleeping and placed on it a piece of paper on which he had written a five-digit number. 'Miss Z' projected herself out of her body while she slept and on waking was able to tell him what the number was.

Both Osis and Tart worked with another psychic, Ingo Swann. Swann was also highly successful at describing pictures and objects placed beyond the range of his normal vision. To test Swann's out-of-the-body vision further, Tart devised what he called an 'optical viewing box'. This box contained a picture which was in fact a cleverly constructed optical illusion. It could only be seen correctly by a person standing in front of the box, looking into it through a small hole. Again, Swann was successful. Once though, he complained that he was unable to see the picture because the inside of the box was too dark. The investigators checked and found he was right – a light placed in the box had failed to work because of a mechanical failure.

All the psychics studied by Osis and Tart were wired up during the experiments to electroencephalographs which record brain activity. The readings from the instruments provided another piece of evidence. They showed a level of brain activity unlike that of the normal sleeping or waking state. This occurred only during the periods when the psychics claimed to be out of the body.

However, some other researchers remained unconvinced. They suggested that a sort of extra-sensory perception might be involved. What the psychics were doing, they claimed, was using clairvoyance, projecting some part of the mind out of the body. To counter this claim, Dr Robert Morris of the Psychical Research Foundation in California devised an ingenious experiment which made use of the reputed psychic sensitivity of animals. His subject, Keith Harary, was asked to project himself into another room where his two kittens were playing and try to attract their attention. The results were extraordinary. At the times when Harry claimed that he was out of the body, the kittens were seen to stop what they were doing and to sit motionless, staring into apparently empty space.

Experiments of this kind have an important bearing on the subject of life after death. No one is claiming OOBEs prove that we survive death, but it does point in that direction. If it can be demonstrated that some part of us can function independently of the physical self, then why shouldn't it continue to do so after the body is dead? Viewed like this, the OOBE may be a rehearsal for death and death itself is a permanent projection! Certainly, people who have had OOBEs have become convinced that the soul exists. D. Scott Rogo, who studied the subject extensively, once wrote, 'I have never met anyone who had an OOBE and is still a materialist.'

The most famous projector of all time was Sylvan Muldoon. His book, *The Projection of the Astral Body*, published in the 1920s, is still the classic work on the subject. Muldoon's first OOBE happened when he was 12 years old, while he was staying with his mother at a spiritualist camp. Later, he attributed the event to the psychic energy generated by the mediums in the building. He dozed off to sleep quite early and woke up with a strange feeling. He was fully conscious but he was rigid, as if stuck to the bed. Then he felt his body vibrating and was aware of buzzing sounds and intense pressure in his head.

> No sooner had the sense of hearing come into being than that of sight followed. When able to see, I was more than astonished! No words could possibly explain my wonderment. I was floating! I was floating in the very air, rigidly horizontal, a few feet above the bed. The room, my exact location, was now comprehended. Things seemed hazy at first, but were becoming clearer. I knew well where I was, yet could not account for my strange behaviour. Slowly, still zigzagging with the strong pressure in the back of my head, I was moving towards the ceiling, all the while horizontal and powerless.
>
> I believed naturally that this was my physical body, as I had always known it, but that it had mysteriously begun to defy gravity. It was too unnatural for me to understand, yet too real to deny – for, being conscious, being able to see, I could not question my sanity. Involuntarily, at about six feet above the bed, as if the movement had been conducted by an invisible force present in the very air, I was uprighted from the horizontal position to the perpendicular, and placed standing upon the floor of the room. There I stood for what seemed to me about two minutes, still powerless to move of my own accord, and staring straight ahead. I was still astrally

cataleptic [a sensation of paralysis]. Then the
controlling force relaxed. I felt free, noticing only the
tension in the back of my head. I took a step, when
the pressure increased for an interval and threw my
body out at an acute angle. I managed to turn
around. There were two of me! I was beginning to
believe myself insane. There was another 'me' lying
quietly upon the bed! It was difficult to convince
myself that this was real, but consciousness would
not allow me to doubt what I saw.

He thought that he had died in his sleep. In a state of panic,
he made his way out of the room, but on attempting to open
the door, he found himself passing through it. Going from
one room to another he tried fervently to arouse the sleeping
occupants of the house. He clutched at them, called to them
and tried to shake them, but his hands passed through them.
They could not even feel his presence. He prowled around
the house in this state for some 15 minutes. Then, to his
intense relief, he felt himself being pulled back into the
body, where he woke with a jolt and a penetrating pain, 'as
if I had been split open from head to foot'.

This vivid account contains many of the features most
commonly associated with the OOBE. It generally begins
with an awareness of leaving the body, either through the
head or, in the majority of cases, floating horizontally upwards towards the ceiling. At this point the projector may
look down and see his own physical body on the bed. The
shock of this usually causes him to come back with an unpleasant jolt. However, the process of leaving the body may
occur unconsciously, in which case the projector wakes up to
find himself floating around in a disembodied state, usually
in his normal physical environment, until he is pulled back
to the body as if he was attached to it by a piece of elastic. It
can, as Muldoon discovered, be a frightening experience. On

the other hand, many people find the sense of freedom from the body to be exhilarating and feel totally at peace.

Personal Experiences

Those of a mediumistic disposition are supposed to have more OOBEs than other people because they are not so firmly anchored in the physical plane. I don't know if this is true. A lot of the mediums I know are surprisingly down-to-earth people. I have had a number of OOBEs and, in the light of what Muldoon says, it is interesting that they have tended to occur more when I have been staying in places where there is a lot of psychic energy or at times when I have been working intensely at a psychic level.

The first time it happened was when I was in my early twenties, the period when I was starting to develop my psychic ability. I had been very tired that night and had gone to bed early, without bothering to wash the dishes, which were piled on the draining board. That wasn't normally something that would have worried me unduly, but on this occasion it must have been playing on my mind or my conscience, because in the middle of the night I found myself going downstairs to the kitchen.

I went over to the sink and began – as I thought – to do the washing up. Then I realised that my hands were going through the dishes without moving them. Strangely enough, I didn't feel frightened by this. The only thought that went through my head was 'This is a waste of time!'. Then I turned round and made my way back upstairs. Everything in the house looked just as it normally did. The only difference was that I was gliding up the stairs rather than walking. As I approached the bedroom door there was a momentary lapse of consciousness, then I woke up and found myself in bed.

It was then that I grasped the fact that I had been out of the body. That was when panic set in. I was paralysed, unable to move a muscle. I was very hot and my heart was beating furiously. I lay still for a few moments. Gradually the paralysis left me and my heartbeat returned to normal. I got up (physically this time) and made myself a cup of tea to help me recover from the shock.

The next occasion was a couple of weeks later. This time I was aware of leaving the body horizontally and rising rapidly into an upright position. I wandered around the house, not walking but floating a few inches above the floor. I was less alarmed than I had been before because in the mean time I had read a number of books on astral projection so I realised what was going on. As with many psychic happenings and experiences, understanding is the key to overcoming fear. Since then I've got quite used to these excursions and, although I don't deliberately seek them, I've come to regard them as part of my psychic life.

Our Spiritual Make-up

The studies that have been made of the OOBE raise an interesting question. What actually is it that leaves the body? To answer this, we need to look at the spiritual composition of human beings.

In the same way that there are various different planes or dimensions of existence, so human beings are composed of various different bodies. These are not something we acquire when we die. They are there all the time, the invisible part of our being. These bodies inter-penetrate, each one vibrating at a different frequency.

The physical body is the lowest and most dense. After this comes the etheric body. This provides the link between

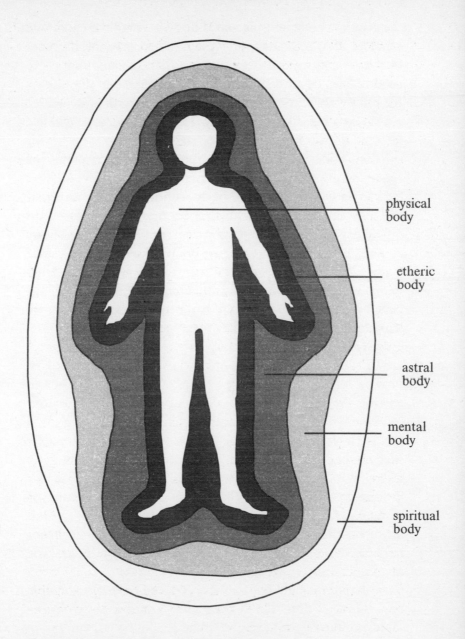

physical
body

etheric
body

astral
body

mental
body

spiritual
body

The different bodies of which we are composed

the physical body and the astral body. It might be called the physical body's life-support system, since part of its function is to draw into the physical body the cosmic energy we need to keep us alive. This energy, called *prana* in the East, is the universal life force that pervades all living things.

Next comes the astral body. This is the body we will live in after death. Beyond this are the mental and the higher spiritual bodies that link us to the more evolved planes of spirit and ultimately to God himself.

In an OOBE the astral body withdraws from the physical. For this reason the phenomenon is sometimes called 'astral projection'. Some psychics can project the astral body at will, but in fact we all have OOBEs every night, since every time we go to sleep the astral body withdraws. Normally, of course, we are blissfully unaware that this has happened. It is when we 'wake up' while out of the body that we have what we call an out-of-the-body experience.

Astral projection does not only take place during sleep. OOBEs also happen to people when they are relaxed or drowsy, or in that half-way state between sleeping and waking. At these times the movement of the astral body out of the physical takes place gently, like a glove sliding off a hand. However, an accident or a blow to the head causes such a shock to the entire system that the astral body is forced out at great speed. Victims of car accidents, for instance, have sometimes said that they were aware of being catapulted forward into the air and were able to look down on the scene of the accident from above, often not realising at first that it was their own body they were looking at.

Meditators may also experience astral projection. People in a state of deep meditation may feel themselves being lifted up out of the body or floating above it. Mediums in trance are sometimes aware of standing outside their physical selves. A healer I know told me that he once found himself, during a healing session, standing at the opposite end of the church, watching himself giving healing to a patient.

OOBEs And NDEs

To me, the most interesting aspect of the OOBE is its close resemblance to the near-death experience. In both cases there is a sense of leaving the body painlessly and floating upwards, hovering near the ceiling. Both projectors and NDEers have reported sensations of freedom and euphoria, have said they were reluctant to return to the body and have lost their fear of death.

Myra Kolber, who is a nurse, told me of an OOBE in which she shared a patient's dying moments:

> I had become very close to a male patient who told me that he knew he had cancer but that I was not to tell the other staff that he knew. I did tell the ward sister who felt that because he trusted me I was to work with him as much as possible. One day we were terribly busy and he called me but I had to say I would see him later but I didn't. That night in my bed asleep I woke up to find myself above my bed near the ceiling, but it wasn't me having the thoughts. The body on the bed was going through the most exhilarating experience of pure joy, the body on the bed and the self above were the same but somehow there was me somewhere seeing all this. Just after this I looked at the clock. It was 12.40 a.m. When I went on duty next morning my patient friend had died at that time. I never spoke about it but I know I experienced his death with him.

As with the NDE, being out of the body gives a good idea
of what it must be like to be an inhabitant of the spirit
world, able to visit this plane of life yet cut off from it.
Muldoon, who became very adept at astral travelling, con-
cluded that, while in this state, he was in effect a ghost. He
could pass through doors and walls, move at great speed
with a gliding or flying motion and could transport himself
from one place to another by the power of thought. His
perception was heightened. He had X-ray vision and could
see things at a distance, but he was seldom able to make
anyone in the physical world aware of his presence. Nor
could he affect physical objects, although he did once, by a
great effort of will, succeed in starting up a metronome.

How can you be sure an OOBE is anything more than a
dream? As with the NDE, this is largely a matter of personal conviction, hard to prove to anyone else. There is a
vividness about the OOBE that is unlike any dream, as
anyone who has had such an experience will testify. More
objective evidence is provided by psychics such as Tanous
and Swann in the experiments described earlier, and there
are many other cases on record where a person has travelled
to a distant place and has subsequently been able to verify
what they saw. Thelma Trenchard from Cornwall wrote to
tell me of just such a case. It happened after she sold her
mother's piano, of which she had been very fond.

Like a good many other people I had had dreams of
floating out of my physical body. I was aware that I
was in another body which was weightless on these
occasions. This time I found myself in my 'light'
body in a room that I did not recognise. I have no
idea how I got there. This room was fairly large.
There seemed to be something round the sides but I
couldn't see what. My attention was not there. The

middle of the room was bare. It had a wooden floor made of long planks with a small, rather faded, carpet in the middle. Somehow or other I now had roller skates on, and I was skating over the boards and carpet and back. My mind was working more clearly than it does in an ordinary state of consciousness. I thought to myself, there is no friction in this state over the boards and carpet so I can go effortlessly. I was as light as a feather and it was lovely. I went on thinking, 'Now I know what it will be like when I die and leave my body behind.' A soundless voice said, 'Remember this, it is important.' I have never skated, nor do I know anyone who does, so that was a most unlikely thing for me to be doing.

About a fortnight after this I was walking down to the village when the lady who had bought the piano happened to be at the front door. She called out to me and said 'Thelma, do come in and see the piano. We've spent £80 on it and it is looking lovely.' So I went in. Her bungalow has been built on the site of an old quarry and there was a basement room below the level of the road which I didn't know existed. She took me down a rather steep ladder to where the piano was. I looked down and with rather a shock I recognised the boards on the floor and the faded carpet. I said, 'What a lovely big room you have down here'. 'Yes', she said, 'when my grandchildren were small we used to clear away the furniture and they used to skate in here'. So I had been acting out what she was going to say to me a fortnight before she actually said it!

Inducing OOBEs

There are various techniques for inducing OOBE, none of which are very easy to master. If you want to try, there are numerous books available that provide detailed instructions (see Bibliography and Recommended Reading). But be warned – it is not something to be undertaken lightly. It can be scary and can impose a strain on the heart. It may also leave you exhausted from lack of sleep!

The technique I would recommend a beginner to try is called the dream method. This was devised by Oliver Fox in the 1920s and is described in his book *Astral Projection*. Fox's method, which is similar to what we today would call lucid dreaming, was to give himself the suggestion, just before going to sleep, that he would become conscious while in the dream. He found that, as soon as he was able to do this, the quality of the dream changed dramatically.

> Instantly the vividness of life increased a
> hundredfold. Never had sea and sky and trees shone
> with such glamorous beauty; even the commonplace
> houses seemed alive and mystically beautiful. Never
> had I felt so absolutely well, so clear-brained, so
> divinely powerful, so inexpressibly *free*! The
> sensation was exquisite beyond words; but it lasted
> only a few moments, and I awoke.

The following method can also be used to induce an OOBE.

▷   Choose a time when it is quiet. The evening is
     ideal, when you are beginning to get drowsy but not
     so tired that you are likely to fall asleep. Find a place
     where you won't be disturbed. Your bedroom is prob-
     ably best. Make sure that there are not going to be
     any noises or distractions. Unplug the phone, shut

the cat outside, and give the family strict instructions that they are not to come in. This is very important, since you will not be able to relax sufficiently if there is any fear of interruption. Make the room dim and ensure that it is warm enough to be comfortable but not too hot.

Lie down on the bed or on a couch and get into a state of total relaxation. Start by curling up your toes, then releasing them. Do the same with the muscles of the feet and ankles. Work your way up your body until every part of you is completely relaxed and at ease. Fix your attention on the ceiling above the bed and picture yourself floating up to touch it. Don't strain, just imagine yourself being gently carried upwards on a cushion of air. You may need to make dozens of attempts before you achieve any result, but eventually you should feel yourself rising horizontally upward, then moving into a vertical position, about 2 or 3 feet away from the bed.

At this point you must keep your nerve! If you panic you will be drawn immediately into the physical body with an unpleasant jolt. If you can remain calm, you can turn round and look at your physical body lying on the bed. You can then begin to explore, but don't be too ambitious at first. Get used to the feeling of moving in the astral body. Walk around the room. Try going out of the room (you will be able to pass through the closed door), and go into other rooms and out of the house into the street.

If you are comfortable with this you can venture further afield but be warned that you probably will not find it very easy. Some books on astral projection give the impression that, once you have learned the technique, you can go off on wonderful and exotic adventures, exploring far-away places. I don't want to be discouraging, and perhaps you are one of those lucky people who have a natural aptitude for this sort of thing, but for most people the reality is rather less spectacular than the books imply. However much you are mentally prepared for it and want it to happen, the shock of finding yourself outside the body is usually enough to cause you to re-enter your physical form at once with great speed. If you do succeed in overcoming this fear you probably won't get much further than your own back garden.

If, after weeks of doing this exercise, you still haven't succeeded don't despair. By practising regularly, you are installing into your subconscious mind the idea of leaving the body and you may well find yourself one night having an OOBE. Success often comes when you least expect it – and when you have given up trying!

▷ You might like to experiment with a friend to see if you can have a shared OOBE. Both you and your friend should practise one or both of the above exercises until you feel you are reasonably proficient at them. Then choose a night when you plan to meet. Pick a place you both know – it might be your friend's bedroom or your own. Concentrate your minds on each other as you do your exercise and will yourself to the place you have chosen or, if your room is the chosen venue, send out your thoughts to draw your friend to you. Even if, when you compare notes the next day, you don't have any conscious memory of meeting, recount any dreams you may have had, and see if they have any features in common.

For anyone who wants to develop their psychic ability, astral projection is well worth studying for the insight it gives into the functioning of your spiritual being. Dreams are another fascinating field of study because they are more than fantasies. They are our doorway into the invisible world.

4

MORE THAN A DREAM

What Are Dreams?

We spend a third of our lives asleep. For those of us who are reluctant to stir from under the covers on cold winter mornings it may be even more. For much of that time we are dreaming. Some people claim that they never dream, but it is only that they can't remember it. Scientific tests have established that everyone dreams several times a night. So what exactly are dreams?

The answer to that question depends upon whether you approach the subject from a psychological or a psychic angle. Obviously, to some extent they are products of our imagination, woven out of the happenings of the day, our thoughts, our desires and fears. They are our subconscious speaking to us and can provide valuable insights, though these may be wrapped up in symbols that are hard to decipher. Some dreams are prophetic or at least give veiled hints of events to come. But dreams contain another element. Sometimes they are confused memories of our travels to the spirit world.

A Psychic View Of Sleep

When we fall asleep the spiritual part of us leaves the physical body to seek refreshment. When this happens we do in fact enter the spirit world which, as we have seen, is not in some distant place but is around us all the time, inter-penetrating our own. During sleep our consciousness rises and falls, touching the many different dimensions and planes of the spirit world. Most of the memories of this are lost on waking. Some impressions are retained, but these are filtered through the subconscious mind, which combines them with its own fantasies. No wonder dreams are often so confusing and defy any psychological interpretation!

Some of the sensations experienced in dreams are caused by the activity of the astral body. Dreams of floating or flying, whatever their Freudian connotations, reflect the movement of the astral as it floats free of the physical body. The subconscious mind registers this movement and incorporates it into a dream, so we may dream that we are flying a plane or floating in a balloon. Dreams of falling are caused when the astral body drops back suddenly into the physical. As the two bodies coincide the jolt wakes us, which is why we always wake up before we hit the ground! If, at the stage when we are just dropping off to sleep, we are startled by a sudden movement or noise, this brings the astral body back abruptly. This is the cause of the jolting sensation, like tripping up a pavement, with which most people are familiar.

Dreams And OOBEs

There is, literally, a world of difference between a dream and an OOBE. In an OOBE the conscious mind is still active.

The projector uses his will-power to release the astral body from the physical but he remains aware of what is going on. When he leaves the body his attention is still fixed on the material plane of life, so he sees the things that are there as physical reality.

OOBEs that occur during sleep are somewhat different. The separation of the astral body from the physical body takes place when the conscious mind is 'switched off' and the sleeper is therefore unaware of what is happening. If the conscious mind 'switches on' again during the projection the sleeper comes to and realises that he is out of the body. He then says that he has had an out-of-the-body experience. Actually, he is only doing what he does every night without his knowledge.

In normal sleep the conscious mind remains dormant. We say we are 'unconscious', but in fact, we are functioning on a different level of consciousness, in which we are in contact with the etheric and astral planes.

Dreams And The Etheric Plane

Chapter 1 described the etheric plane as the borderland between our physical world and the world of the spirit. It might be called the dreamland of the astral world. It is also our dreamland. As we drift along through this plane in sleep we pick up its fleeting sight and sounds, but since consciousness is dim here, everything is shadowy and distorted. Here we may encounter people who, like us, are asleep and out of the body. We may also meet spirit people but we will not have any clear contact with them. We pass each other like ships on a foggy night, only vaguely aware of each other's existence.

We have seen that, after death, souls pass through the

etheric plane on their way to the spirit world. It is a similar situation with sleep. We may pass the whole night on the etheric level. But sometimes our consciousness rises to the level of the astral world, where the mind becomes lucid. It is as if we had passed beyond death. Once again, we usually forget all about it on waking. As we return to the body we have to descend through the etheric and that tends to obliterate memory, like wiping a tape. But some people who have trained themselves in the art of astral projection have used it as a means of exploring the spirit world.

Accounts of the explorations are remarkably like those of NDEers and spirit communicators. They speak of the beauty of the environment and of its similarity to the earth in an idyllic form. One of the best-known writers on the subject is Robert Munroe, who recounted his adventures in *Journeys Out of the Body*.

Munroe's Locales

Munroe identifies three distinct locations. The first of these, which he calls 'Locale I', he defines as 'the here-now'. This is the ordinary physical world. Though he is sometimes able to travel many miles from his own home, to visit people on the physical plane and even on occasions to make them aware of his presence, he seldom encounters anything or anyone of a spiritual nature. On this physical level he experiences the type of OOBE with which researchers are familiar. Though he is in the astral body his consciousness is directed towards the material world, so that is what he sees.

Sometimes he finds himself in a very different environment, which he terms 'Locale III'. This is a puzzling region, similar to the earth yet not quite like it, peopled by men and women living ordinary lives. He is unable to decide where this location is and I do not know of any other astral traveller who claims to have found it. He speculates that it may be some sort of parallel universe, but I believe that it may be one of the numerous regions of the astral, since we are told that some of the planes near the earth are surprisingly like our world.

He describes passing through the etheric, which he experiences as 'a misty place' where he comes into contact with other sleepers as well as with those who have died and have not yet progressed into the astral. Here he also sees demonic beings, for, as he discovers, parts of the etheric have a hell-like aspect, which no doubt give rise to some of our bad dreams and nightmares.

But beyond the mists he enters what he calls 'Locale II'. This is immediately identifiable as the astral or spirit world.

> To me, it was a place or condition of pure peace, yet
> exquisite emotion. It was as if you were floating in
> warm soft clouds where there is no up or down,
> where nothing exists as a separate piece of matter.
> The warmth is not merely around you, it is of you
> and through you. Your perception is dazzled and
> overwhelmed by the Perfect Environment.

He comments that this world resembles the earth in many ways but that time as we know it does not exist there. All the artifacts, and indeed the whole environment, are created by the power of thought. Once, he found himself in park-like surroundings where hundreds of men and women, all strangers to him, were strolling by, some dazed, some calm and some apprehensive. He learned that this was a reception area where those who had recently died were met by friends and relatives, and taken to the place where they belonged.

The beauty of this world moved him greatly. It seemed to him as if he had come home. He speaks of his reluctance to return to the body and the intense nostalgia he suffered for days afterwards. He concludes that the astral world is our natural environment and that, as soon as the astral body leaves the physical it will, unless it is held back by the pull of the earthly mind, make its way back there.

NDEers have similarly said that they were unwilling to leave the astral world and come back to earth. And that is one reason why we need to sleep. Like a diver coming up for air, we need to return to our spirit home for refreshment. Sometimes we do partially remember and wake up with the sense that we have been somewhere beautiful – if only we could recall where! But perhaps it is as well that the return through the etheric level does blot out the memory, or it would be hard to be content in this world, which is so unappealing by comparison.

Astral Meetings

While we are in the sleep state we frequently meet those we know in spirit. These meetings take place in different ways and upon different dimensions. They can bring great comfort but they are often puzzling because we remember only disjointed fragments. An interesting story was sent to me by Pamela Emson, who met her grandmother in what seemed an incredibly vivid dream.

> I felt myself moving in a downward direction for a few seconds, then I found that I was outside, a short distance from where my grandmother had lived. It was dark and I was surprised to find myself there. I then realised that my body was not with me and I was a ball of light, about 8 or 9 inches in diameter. I was hovering about 4 feet from the ground. At first I was not sure what to do but I quickly realised that I could move in any direction, just by thought. I began

moving forward very quickly and was amazed by the speed. I felt the wind around me. I followed the road and went to my grandmother's house. At the door I hesitated – it was open just as she always left it when she expected me, but I knew that she had died. However, I wanted to see her, so I went in. I was puzzled to see that the house, which I had cleared with my mother, was exactly the same as when my grandmother had lived there. I think at this stage that I became more like the 'me' I am used to, with a body, but I am not sure. I called to her, as I normally would, and she replied as usual, 'Come in dear, I'm in the kitchen'. I waited in the living room and after a few moments my grandmother came in. She stood before me and I was so pleased to see her. She said, 'Do I look the same?' I replied that she did, the only difference was her size – she was much bigger. I told her this and she replied that she had not done this before. She gradually became smaller, until she was nearer her normal size. We spent what seemed like quite a long time together and I know that we talked but sadly, I cannot remember what about. I wish I could. After a while I became aware of the strangeness of the situation and a wave of panic came over me. I told my grandmother that I was feeling scared and I would have to go. She stood up and said, 'Before you go I want you to meet someone'. She turned and beside her was a woman who smiled at me. She was very still and not as 'real' as my grandmother, as if I was looking at her through smoked glass. I am fairly sure, from photographs, that she was my grandmother's sister, who died four years before I was born. On seeing this, my panic took over and I left. I remember leaving the house as a ball of light, then nothing.

This story illustrates how confusing these meetings often are. I feel sure that Pamela really did meet her grandmother but there seems to be a dream element involved, or perhaps her grandmother had recreated, by her thoughts, the house in which she used to live – who knows?

The astral meetings tend to occur most vividly and most frequently in the period immediately following the death of a loved one. This is not surprising, since at that time the person will still be very close to the earth and possibly anxious to get in contact with those they have left behind. This may be their best, in fact their only, way of communicating. In our normal waking state we are unaware of their presence but when we leave the body and rise on to the astral plane on which they are dwelling we can meet with no barrier between. The difficulty, from their point of view, must be to get us to remember it in the morning!

Dreams and astral meetings can be blended together in a very confusing way as our consciousness fluctuates between one level and another. One sitter described to me how she had had what she called a 'dream that was more than a dream' about her father, who had died a short while before and to whom she had been very attached.

'I could see him in the distance,' she told me, 'and I knew he was trying to say something to me but I couldn't make out the words. I seemed to be in a fog. The more I tried to reach him, the further away he got. Do you think I really saw him?'

I couldn't tell her for sure. It is often impossible to separate dreams from reality and, of course, many dreams are no more than the product of our imagination. As with the OOBE, the person concerned has to be guided by their own intuitive sense of what is true. In this particular case, however, my feeling is that the sitter did see her father but that, as her consciousness was operating on the etheric level (the fog she described), she was unable to communicate with him clearly.

Experiences Of The Spirit World

On those rare occasions when we do have a glimpse of the spirit world in sleep, and bring back a clear memory, it is a beautiful experience and one that is never forgotten.

Mary Poulton had an experience that changed her life. Her 23-year-old brother had been killed in an accident and Mary, who was very close to him, was unable to come to terms with his death. She was told by a medium that she had to stop her excessive grieving and let her brother go so that he could progress.

> A few weeks later I had a dream. I call it a dream although I don't know whether I was asleep or awake. I saw a man in a white robe standing by the bed. He said, 'I'm going to take you to see where your brother is going to live!' Within seconds, I found myself in a beautiful place, like the garden of a convent. There were nuns there. One of them said to me, 'This is where your brother will be coming to rest. He will be looked after here, but first you must let him go.' The nun said that she was going to leave me alone for a little while. I could look around the place, but I was not to go beyond a certain boundary which she indicated in the distance.

Of course, Mary's curiosity got the better of her and she couldn't resist going to see what lay beyond the boundary. In contrast to the garden, it was a bleak, barren place. Later, she learned that this must have been one of the lower regions of the astral, but at that time she had no such knowledge. In a panic, she called out to the nun, who led her back to the garden. Then the man in the robe came and took her back home.

I could see the room and see myself lying on the bed. I felt myself slipping back into the body. The man said to me, 'Some time in the future we will meet again'. After that, I was a different person. I was able to stop grieving for my brother and feeling sorry for myself.

At that time, Mary knew nothing of mediumship but, many years later, when she began to work as a medium, she saw the man again. He was, and still is, one of the spirit helpers who works with her.

Shortly after my father died I had an experience that was so real that although it was over 20 years ago, it has stayed with me to this day. I was walking down a dark, narrow road which I know was the etheric borderland. There were dim figures all around me which made me nervous and I began to run. Then I realised that my grandmother, who had died when I was seven, was beside me. This calmed me and we went along together.

Suddenly the scene lit up as though someone had switched on a powerful light. I came out into beautiful countryside. Everything was radiantly alive. The birds had exotic plumage of vivid colours. There was a feeling of vast expanse, freedom and peace. Then I saw my father standing there. I was so overjoyed that I threw my arms around him. He was quite real and substantial, and looking just as I remembered him before he had become ill. We talked for a while though I don't remember what we said. He introduced me to someone I had never met. I put out my hand to shake hands with this person ... then suddenly I woke up in bed, wishing I could have stayed there for ever.

Those who are psychically aware do tend to go astral travelling more frequently and to remember it more because their thoughts are attuned to the spiritual dimension and, as the astral body is directed by the power of thought, their thoughts will take them there. But you don't need to be a medium or a psychic to have experiences of this kind. Love is the basis of all spirit communication and, where there is a tie of affection between someone on earth and someone in the spirit world, this bond will draw them together.

However, the thoughts that are in your mind as you are falling asleep greatly influence where you go and what you experience on the spirit planes, so if you want to meet your loved ones in the astral and to retain the memory of your meeting, you need to prepare yourself.

▷ Try to spend a few minutes before you go to bed meditating. (A meditation exercise is given in Chapter 7.) Consciously let go of the cares and worries of the day and let your mind be calm and peaceful. Send out your thoughts to those you love in the spirit world and ask them to be with you.

You might care to experiment with Fox's technique for inducing astral projection described at the end of Chapter 3. Will yourself to 'wake up' during the dream and see what happens.

Dream Diaries

Anyone can train themselves to remember their dreams, if they have sufficient patience and determination. The exercise is well worth the effort because dreams have so much to teach us, both in their psychological and their psychic aspects.

A good way to start is to keep a dream diary. Have a notebook by your bed and, as soon as you wake up in the morning, or if you wake during the night, write down all you can recall of your dreams. It doesn't matter how fragmentary or trivial it is. The object is to get your mind into the habit of remembering everything that occurs in the dream state.

An alternative method is to have a tape recorder beside you and speak into it, then you can write up your notes at leisure during the day. This often works better since dreams are such fragile things, and the mere act of sitting up and reaching for your pen and paper can drive them completely out of your head.

At first when you start keeping your diary you may have very little to put in it. Some nights you may remember nothing at all. But if you persevere you will gradually start to remember more and more, and your dreams will take on a more vivid quality.

Dreams and astral travel demonstrate that we are more than the physical body, more than the brain. We are like icebergs. Only the tip, the conscious mind and the physical body, is perceptible to our normal sense. Below the surface are depths greater than we can ever plumb. Whether we acknowledge it or not, we are all in touch with the spiritual dimension. To prove this to ourselves we do not have to take classes in psychic development or lose ourselves in profound meditation. We only have to open our spiritual eyes.

5

Nearer Than Hands
And Feet

Have you ever felt a presence, heard a supernatural voice or seen a spirit being? If so, you are not unusual. These spontaneous contacts with the spirit world happen more frequently than you might think, not only to psychics but also to people who consider themselves completely materialistic and don't even believe in life after death. The spirit world is around us all the time, inter-penetrating our own. We enter it whenever we go to sleep and, in any case, we are linked to it because we are in our essence spirit beings underneath these physical overcoats. So it doesn't require much, just a slight opening of the mind, a small shift in consciousness, for the veil to lift, giving us a glimpse of the higher dimension.

Young children often have a natural awareness of the spirit world. Their imaginary playmates may be spirit children. It's not uncommon for a child to see, for example, a deceased grandparent and to chat away to them quite happily. It's only when they tell the adults around them and receive a horrified reaction that they start to be afraid.

When I was young I was frequently aware of spirit presences. My grandmother died when I was seven but to me it was as if she was still around. I used to talk to her in my mind and tell her my troubles, just as I had done when she was on earth. I never heard her answer but I was sure she heard me and understood. I wasn't afraid of her; her presence was warm and comforting. This contact seemed perfectly natural to me but my family were alarmed when I told them about it, so I resolved never to speak about it again.

As adults, it is fear that seals us off from the spirit dimension. That, and the refusal to believe that it exists, sets up a barrier that cripples the psychic senses. But sometimes the invisible world breaks through the barrier. This can be caused by intense emotion, by the longing to reach someone on the other side of life or by their longing to reach someone here. Or it may happen when we are relaxed, because then the mind drops its guard and impressions can filter through.

Seeing Spirit People

There are many kinds of contact with the spirit world, ranging from full-blown visions to the vague, hard to define sensing of a presence. The most obvious example is seeing a ghost, as happened to Joy Cooke, who saw a mysterious woman while staying in a cottage her parents had rented for the summer.

> We had to collect the keys from the estate agent in the pretty, countrified little village 'a stone's throw away from the sea' and he said 'I'm sure you'll love the place, it has been well looked after. The owner left it to her life-long friends – three sisters who lived nearby – and they go there every day to open the windows and look after the garden.'

As soon as we saw the picturesque thatched cottage it was love at first sight! We were met at the gate by a bright-eyed lady who said 'Come along in. I'll show you around.' We could see one of the sisters weeding the garden; she gave us a friendly smile.

Upstairs, as my mother chatted with the lady, I walked over to the bedroom window and looked out over the large garden. In the far corner was a natural pool and sitting on a bench under a weeping willow tree was an elderly lady wearing a large straw sunhat, nursing a Pekinese.

When we went back to the estate agent to return the keys and book the holiday cottage, he said, 'Yes, everyone in the village was sad when old Mrs Sanderson died – she was quite a character you know – every day she would walk around that garden wearing a sunhat, no matter what the weather, and she would not go anywhere without her little Pekinese.'

Ghosts of the traditional sort, such as headless ladies and hooded monks, are actually in very short supply in our technological age. Most ghosts are, like Joy Cooke's, ordinary men and women who lived on earth in the recent past. I never describe them as 'ghosts', since the word evokes an attitude of disbelief mixed with fear. I prefer to call them spirit people because that's what they are – people who retain very human feelings and characteristics, and whose dimension of life is only one small step removed from our own.

They certainly don't mean us any harm, but all the same, it is very startling to suddenly see one. It still startles me and I'm a medium! In the days when I first started to develop my mediumship this used to happen to me a lot. I would be walking down a street, for instance, not even thinking about anything psychic, when suddenly I would see someone standing in front of me. It would only be for an instant but for that time they looked so real and solid that I didn't realise they weren't flesh and blood – until they vanished just as suddenly. I was puzzled as to why this should occur. Why should these people appear when I was least expecting it and not in my development circle, when I was actually trying to see? And why should I see strangers rather than those like my father and grandmother, whom I knew to be close to me?

It was an elderly medium I consulted who supplied the answer. She explained that, if you are naturally psychic, especially if you are not using your psychic ability, the energy will build up from time to time like steam pressure in a kettle. You then will experience a momentary flash of awareness which seems to come completely out of the blue. What you see or hear at these times is entirely due to chance. You may see someone you knew very well and wonder why they chose that particular moment to manifest themselves to you. Actually, they are probably there frequently but you are not normally aware of them, and most likely they are as surprised to be seen as you are to see them. But you might as easily see a stranger, not because they have any significance for you but because they just happen to be there at the time.

What these momentary spurts of psychic energy do is to raise your level of consciousness so as to bring it into line with the spiritual dimension. Natural mediums are born with an automatic hot-line to the spirit world. In fact, they may be unable to shut off their awareness and have difficulty in anchoring themselves in this world. Some mediums who are not so well tuned in to start with have to learn how to increase their perception.

John McCormack got the surprise of his life when, in one of these momentary flashes, he saw his grandmother.

I loved my grandmother very much and she loved me, but we had fallen out and she stopped talking to me. I had displeased her by something I had done when I was 16 years old. She was a grudge carrier, unfortunately, and rebuffed my many attempts to make up with her. She died several years later in November 1954, when I was in the US army in Germany. I felt very bad about her dying before we had a chance to be reconciled. Evidently she did too, because she came back.

One bright, warm, sunny Saturday at the end of May or beginning of June 1956, about 11 o'clock in the morning, I was walking along a busy street in New York. I was heading for a nearby café to get breakfast. As I walked along, I casually glanced to my right at the roadway, the passing cars and the shops and the people across the road, all in the sun. The road was perhaps 40 or 50 feet wide, room for two lanes of parked cars and four lanes of moving traffic. Directly across from me, standing at the edge of the footpath on the far side of the road, was my grandmother. Well, that stopped me dead in my tracks. There she stood with her shopping cart, and her black hat and coat and black shoes – just the way she always looked when she went shopping. She never looked directly at me, thanks be to God, because I was decidedly nervous at that stage.

Now that particular street was a busy one, but I seemed to have lost awareness of the traffic from that moment on. I don't remember seeing any cars pass by in either direction. Just my grandmother standing there, waiting to cross. Then she started across and I nearly died! I could feel the hair on my neck and head standing straight out. Fortunately for my heart, she did not come straight across the road, but walked

to my left (her right) at an angle, staying the same
distance from me on my side of the road, crossed it,
and went into the F.W. Woolworth shop in which my
mother was working at the time. As soon as my
grandmother was out of sight, I spun on my heels
and ran around the corner into the nearest pub!

Some time after that he began to hear her calling his name.
This would happen at night when everything was quiet or
when he was thinking of nothing in particular. Eventually
he decided that she was trying to tell him she was sorry for
the quarrel they had had, so he spoke to her, saying that he
loved and forgave her. After that he never saw or heard from
her again.

We have seen that the dead come back for many
reasons and sometimes, like John McCormack's grandmother, they want to say they are sorry for something they
did on earth, or to make their peace with someone with
whom they had a quarrel. They may feel deep remorse over
the hurt they have caused, especially as they have clearer
insights after death, and are better able to understand the
effect of their words and actions on others.

Frequently, when I am giving a sitting, a communicator
will come back full of regrets. A man who had walked out
on his family came through to his daughter, bitterly regret-
ting that he had ruined her life. His daughter was going
through a similar situation; her husband of many years had
just left her. She was able to forgive her father for the first
time and he promised to do all he could to help her.

Another sitter was less responsive when I brought her
mother to her.

'She was very unkind to me when she was alive,' she
told me coldly, 'and I don't want to hear from her now, so
you can just tell her to go away!'

Perhaps she had good reason to feel as she did but I

thought it a pity that she should harden her heart in this way. I could feel her mother's sorrow and sense of rejection. Had she felt able to forgive, it would have brought them both peace of mind.

A person who has died suddenly will often feel a great anxiety to get in touch with those left behind. Their sudden departure will have come as a shock to them as well. So often sitters who have suffered an unexpected loss say to me, 'If only we had had the chance to say goodbye!' The person in spirit usually feels the same. They need to express their love and to say the words that were left unsaid. They may also wish to give practical advice to do with sorting out their affairs.

NDEers have described what it is like to be able to see people on earth but to be unable to make themselves seen or heard. Those who have died experience a similar frustration when they know their families are grieving for them and cannot let them know that they are still alive in another dimension. It helps them greatly if they are able to make contact and their presence is acknowledged. The spirit world is more beautiful and much happier than this, but the spirit people are still their old, very human selves and feel the same emotions that we feel.

Detecting A Spirit Presence

You don't need to be especially gifted to detect a spirit presence in your home. It happens all the time. The awareness comes in various ways. You may see something out of the corner of your eye and when you turn to look there is no one there. Or you may hear a voice calling your name, either as an external sound or a voice in your head. Other common signs are the sense of being watched or the whiff of a familiar smell.

Occasionally there may be psychic phenomena in the house, such as noises or small objects being moved. I am not talking here of poltergeist activity, which is something altogether different and may be malicious. If you have a spirit who is throwing the furniture around, call in a competent medium without delay. What I am referring to – and again, this is much more common than you might suppose – are those puzzling little sounds and movements, clicks and rattles or flowers moving when there is no breeze.

One woman told me that she smelled her late father's tobacco in his room, months after he had died. Another recounted how she found her partner's picture on the wall hanging crooked every time she went into the room. Each time she straightened it but a couple of minutes later it would be crooked again. This had never happened before his death, and it ceased as soon as she spoke to him aloud and told him she knew he was there. Yet another sitter said that she found a ring her husband had given her on top of a cupboard, where she could only reach it by standing on a chair. She had misplaced the ring several times before and felt that this was his way of warning her to take care if it. A woman whose young daughter had died found a flower, out of a vase of flowers she had placed on her sideboard in the child's memory, taken out of the vase and placed carefully by its side.

There is no need to be afraid of any of these things. Assuming that you have checked to eliminate any natural explanation, accept that they are indications your spirit loved ones are around. To move objects in this way they need to draw on the psychic power that is available in the house, so you will be more likely to experience this sort of manifestation if you or anyone you live with has a lot of psychic energy. How they produce smells and perfumes, I really don't know. There are still many things about the spirit world we don't understand. I am quite at a loss, for instance, to account for the curious story told to me by Ernest Mayes of Yorkshire.

Mr Mayes's brother Norman died in 1991. His brother's wife ordered the headstone. It was the type you can see in any undertaker's window, with a spray of flowers and the monogram 'IHS' inscribed on the top left-hand corner. (The IHS motif is frequently used on tombstones and other Christian monuments – the letters stand for the Hebraic version of the words inscribed on the Cross, Jesus of Nazareth, King of the Jews.) As many people will be aware, when you order a tombstone it comes with the design already engraved. All the monumental masons do is add the name of the deceased person and any other inscription requested by the family. But when the tombstone arrived, Mr Mayes and his sister-in-law could hardly believe their eyes, for instead of the IHS monogram were the initials, 'N.M.'. The monumental masons were contacted and were mystified as to how the pre-prepared part of the design had been changed; they were certainly not responsible. They offered to change it back but the family decided to leave it as it was. What makes the story even more intriguing is that, while he was alive, Norman Mayes was in the habit of putting his initials on many of his personal possessions.

Deathbed Visions

The hour of death is a time when the spirit and physical worlds draw very close together. Dying people sometimes see friends or relatives coming to greet them and help them into the spirit world. Deathbed visions, as they are called, have been studied by parapsychologists. The most famous study was carried out by Dr Karlis Osis whose work on OOBEs proved so positive. Dr Osis published his research in 1961, under the title *Deathbed Observations by Physicians and Nurses*. He demonstrated that the patients concerned were fully conscious and in a lucid state of mind. A few of them reported seeing relatives they did not even know had died. Some had visions of a beautiful land, their descriptions matching those of NDEers who glimpsed the spirit world. These spirit visitors and the visions remove the fear of death and make the transition to the next world easier.

People who are keeping vigil by the bedside of a dying person may also sense the closeness of spirit, becoming themselves highly perceptive and seeing the same spirit visitors or hearing music from another world. Dorothy Chapman, a medium from Surrey, was brought into spiritualism by an experience she had when her father-in-law was dying.

The nurse had told us the crisis would be that night, so my husband Charlie and I sat up all night with him. At about half-past-two my father-in-law started fighting for his life. Charlie had fallen asleep and so had my mother-in-law. I was the only one awake.

I could hear a lot of shouting coming from the garden, people calling to each other and laughing as if they had just come out of the pub. I thought, if they don't stop soon I'm going to go out there and complain! Then I turned round and looked through the glass door that led out into the hall. There were three little boys standing at the bottom of the stairs. Other people were gathering in the hall, running from all directions to stand behind them. Then I heard music, the most beautiful music I had ever heard. It went on for a long time then gradually it faded away. As it did so, my husband woke up. My father-in-law slipped away peacefully a few hours later.

Traditionally, ghosts are supposed to appear at the moment of their death, usually to some poor, startled victim miles away who only later learns that the person died at that precise moment. This is the stuff of which ghost stories are made but it has some basis in fact. The literature of parapsychology is full of examples which have been given the name of 'crisis apparitions'. Brenda Marshall, the former president of the College of Psychic Studies in Kensington, wrote in the college journal *Light* about her husband's death.

> About five years ago in the early evening, while in my sitting room, I experienced a strange lassitude. This persisted most strongly. It was unlike ordinary tiredness and I remained in this state of peaceful expectancy for almost two hours. The moment I lay down in bed I had a brief sensation, still clearly remembered, of achievement, a satisfying hint of some goal attained; and then, letting go to a welcoming haze. My husband was on a ship on his way to South America and I had no reason to suppose that anything untoward was happening. It was not until next morning that the telegram came saying he had died most unexpectedly *at that time* the previous day, and I learnt later that he had stayed in his cabin, saying he felt tired.

It is not hard to understand why these things happen. When a person is dying their thoughts go out to someone they love, with a strong desire to be with them. As the astral body moves by the power of thought, this desire immediately carries them to where their longing is directed. Their feeling is so intense that the person to whom the feeling is directed picks up a mental contact or is able to see them. As the astral body is a replica of the physical, the spirit will usually appear as they did on earth, but sometimes the astral form may be seen as a mist, which is no doubt why ghosts were believed to float around in shrouds!

I have said that it is in the few days after a person has died that those who are left behind tend to feel their presence most strongly. This is very understandable in simple human terms. Although everyone is met when they die and is taken to the spirit world, they are bound to feel concern for those they have left on earth. I have already spoken of their need to reassure their families that they are still alive, and to sort out any unfinished business and give comfort to those who are grieving. This need will draw them back to those they love and to their familiar surroundings. It takes a while to adjust to being what we call dead!

When A Loved One Has Recently Died

So what should you do, if you have lost someone dear to you and you can still feel them close?

▷ First of all, don't be afraid. They are still the same person, not a ghost. Talk to them in your mind, or aloud if you prefer and let them know that you are aware of them. Book a sitting with a good medium to give them an opportunity to communicate with you. If you want to place flowers in the cemetery or garden of remembrance do so, but there is really no need. Their spirit is not buried under the ground. They are with you wherever you are, so why not put flowers in your home, where they can see and enjoy them?

Make a few minutes every day, perhaps in the evening when everything is quiet, to sit calmly and send out your thoughts to your loved one. Remember that, if you are missing them, they are also missing you and would love, just as much as you, to be able to give you a hug and a kiss or sit down and have a chat. Don't expect to see them suddenly appear or to hear them speaking with your physical ears. In fact, at first you may not feel that you are making any contact at all. But, in time, if you persevere, you will become aware that you are getting through. This will not come in any obvious way and your disbelieving family will probably still think you are having hallucinations, but don't let them put you off. You will feel the contact, like a warm inner glow. Once you have felt it, you will know that true spirit communication feels different from thoughts produced by your own mind. But it is a difference that cannot be defined – you must experience it for yourself.

Be prepared for the fact that your awareness will fluctuate. Sometimes you will feel that you are getting through, while at other times your mind will be a blank. Don't strain on the blank days. Just allow yourself to be still. And take note of your dreams. Remember that dreams can be memories of meetings on the astral plane.

There are bound to be times when you feel sad. This emotion needs to be expressed. Mourning has been likened to amputation. It takes time to heal. Even feelings of which you are ashamed, such as abandonment, resentment and anger, need to be allowed release rather than being bottled up, since only by admitting to such emotions can they be worked through and eventually overcome. I am sure those in spirit understand these needs. When we cry, they cry with us but they are healing tears, and the love from those in the next world sustains us and brings us up through the shadows into the light again.

How long this strong sense of presence lasts depends on the individual and on the strength of their bond with loved ones on earth. Some people remain close for years, waiting until it is time for the one they love to join them in the spirit world. Others may be off very quickly – they cannot wait to get on with the adventure of a new life!

If you are sensitively attuned to the one you love, you will feel after a time that there is something different about them. The love and the care are still there, but it is as if they have moved on to a higher level of consciousness. You will feel a greater light and joy about them. When this happens – and you will know it with that inner knowing – do not try to hold them back by asking them to stay with you or by constantly seeking 'messages' from them through mediums. As they progress, so they can bring you more light and love because they themselves are learning and growing. Take strength from their presence, but let it be a strength that enables you to live this life to the full instead of clinging to the past.

In fact, you will never lose touch with them completely. There will be times, such as special anniversaries, when they will once again draw very close. It is a nice idea to mark their birthday or the anniversary of their death in some way, perhaps by placing flowers for them in the home. They will be aware of your needs and will do their best to help whenever they sense that you are in need of comfort or guidance. This guidance comes in strange, subtle ways that make you wonder, was someone looking after me or was it just coincidence?

A medium I know, Gwen Bisp, gave me a typical example of this. She needed some repairs done to her house but didn't have much money to spare and couldn't find a reliable builder. Being reluctant to pick a name at random from the *Yellow Pages*, she sought help of her husband in spirit. Not long after, she was asked to give healing to a small boy. The boy's father turned out to be a builder and offered to do the job very cheaply for her. Although she doesn't charge for healing, Gwen accepts donations, and the amount of money she had received that day was the exact sum needed to pay the bill.

I always ask for help whenever I have a problem and somehow things work out every time. I will 'just happen' to bump into someone who can assist me, or someone whose behaviour has been giving me difficulties will have an unexpected change of heart. I can't, of course, prove that any of this is due to intervention from the other side of life, but it happens too often to be mere chance.

Asking For Guidance

There is much the spirit world can do to smooth our pathway. You should not expect them to live your life for you, or to make decisions that it is your responsibility to make for yourself, but if you have a problem and you ask sincerely, very often the help will come.

▷ Once again, sit quietly and make your mind as still and quiet as you can. Send out your thoughts to those you love, or whom you feel to be close to you, and ask them to guide you. There is no need to explain your troubles to them – they will already know. Try to be aware of any thoughts that come into your head but, if nothing comes, don't feel that they are not answering you. It may be that you are straining too hard to hear, and any strain in your mind will create a mental block that they cannot penetrate.

The answer may come later, when you are relaxed.

A thought will drop into your mind or maybe some unexpected solution will present itself. The more you develop your intuitive powers (some exercises to help you to do this are given in Chapter 8), the more you will be able to receive guidance in this way. It may not always come – some problems cannot be solved. But at least you may receive insights that will help you to deal with them in a more constructive way.

There is no great gulf fixed between this world and the next. Those we love are 'closer than breathing, nearer than hands and feet'. I am not saying that this knowledge makes it easy to get over the death of someone you love. You wouldn't be human if you didn't miss having them around. But with this knowledge, grief can have a healing and transforming effect. I meet many people who have suffered bereavement, and I am constantly surprised and moved to see how many of them come through it enriched and strengthened. Because they have viewed death in a spiritual perspective, seeing it as a new beginning for the person who has died, it has become a new beginning for them also. They have discovered spiritual gifts in themselves which they never realised they possessed, and have gone on to become mediums, healers or teachers, helping others to find the same comfort they have found.

Tessa Hughes expressed this to me beautifully. Her fiancé John died very suddenly after what should have been a routine hip replacement operation. Her world was turned upside down and she saw nothing but darkness ahead, yet knowing that he was with her, and with his help, she was able gradually to build her life again. Now, seven years later, she admits that at times she is still swamped by feelings of sadness and anger, and finds it desperately hard to cope with life without him. But she found her grief to be a time of personal growth. Today she works as a healer, empowering other people to heal their own spirits. Because of what she has learned she is able to write as follows:

> I realise more than anything that I am a much finer person having experienced this love, and that any loss opens up grief which has never been grieved before, so that I am probably still working through the tears of all my life – and ultimately that is a deep and powerful healing process. Of course, when I hurt – and I do – I am really angry that he died and put me through all this, but you can't turn the clock back.
>
> It has to have been the most enriching experience of my life . . . the greatest grief is also the greatest opportunity.

I hope the advice I have given in this chapter will be of some comfort if you are suffering a recent bereavement and will help you to be aware that your loved one is still close. Later, I will be explaining in detail how to develop this awareness further, perhaps becoming a medium yourself. But before that I want to look at the objective evidence for life after death. There is a great mass of this, from many different sources. And some of it is extremely hard to refute.

6

FINDING THE
EVIDENCE

I have often been asked what is the most convincing evidence for life after death I have ever come across. This is a question I find hard to answer, not for any lack of material but because there is so much that it is difficult to know where to begin. One of the most interesting cases I have encountered was related to me by a London spiritualist, Elsie McLeod.

Elsie had regular sittings for a number of years with the famous medium Leslie Flint. Leslie, who died recently, has featured in my other books. He was called a 'physical' medium. That is to say, he was able to produce something called ectoplasm. This is a strange, proto-plasmic substance that is exuded from the medium's body during seances and is used by the spirit operators to move or levitate objects, or else can be moulded into materialised forms. In Leslie's case, it was used to produce a 'voice-box', a device through which the communicators could speak and make their voices audible to the sitters. Hundreds of sitters were able to converse in this way with their spirit loved ones and their tales would be enough to fill a book, but Elsie's story was exceptional.

Elsie had a friend, a Mrs Foulds, who was also her hairdresser. She knew that, as a child, Mrs Foulds had been imprisoned in the dreaded Auschwitz concentration camp and that her sufferings there had been so awful that she would never talk about them. One day while she was having her hair done the conversation turned to psychic matters and Elsie recalled a sitting with Leslie Flint, many years before, at which a woman had come through speaking with a German accent who said her name was Dr Anna Gaster and that she had perished at Auschwitz. Elsie asked Mrs Foulds whether she had known Dr Gaster. Mrs Foulds replied that she had and that she remembered her with gratitude. The doctor had saved both Mrs Foulds and her sister, hiding them on several occasions when Dr Mengele, the so-called 'angel of death', was doing his rounds. Elsie asked her if she would like to listen to a tape-recording of the sitting. Mrs Foulds agreed, and both she and her sister were able to identify the doctor's voice.

Evidence of this kind is hard to dispute. Dr Gaster was completely unknown to the medium or any of the sitters present at that time. Elsie's friend had not even mentioned the name to her, yet both Mrs Foulds and her sister recognised the voice of the long-dead doctor.

There are hundreds of cases on record which are just as difficult to explain away as telepathy, ESP or any other possible cause. In fact, to quote Colin Wilson, a leading writer on the occult and the paranormal, 'the sheer volume of physical evidence for survival after death is so immense that to ignore it is like standing at the foot of Mount Everest and insisting that you cannot see a mountain.'

Much of this evidence has been collected by the Society for Psychical Research (SPR). Founded in 1882 by a group of Cambridge academics, the SPR set itself the task of investigating physical phenomena of every kind, from the dramatic happenings in the seance room (this was the period when spiritualism was in its heyday), to hauntings and telepathy. Meticulous notes were kept of every case they studied, and the results were published in their *Journal* and *Proceedings*, as well as in several weighty tomes including *Phantasms of the Living* and F.W.H. Myers's *Human Personality and its Survival of Bodily Death*. The following examples are taken from Myers's book.

In 1876 a commercial traveller was staying at a hotel in the city of St Joseph, Minnesota, USA. It was high noon and the sun was shining brightly. He was sitting at a table not thinking of anything in particular when he became conscious that someone was sitting on his left. Turning, he saw in a brief flash an apparition of his sister, who had died some nine years before. As he called her name the apparition vanished, but not before he had noticed something strange; a bright red scratch mark on the right side of her face. So startled was he that he took the next train home and told his parents what had happened. His mother fainted in surprise. She explained how she had accidently made the scratch mark while laying out her daughter after death, a fact which she had mentioned to no living person.

In 1891 a farmer called Conley from Iowa, USA, was found dead in an outhouse. He was carried to the morgue where his filthy old clothes were thrown aside and the body prepared for shipment to his home. His son collected the corpse but when the man's daughter was told of his death she fell into a swoon. On recovering she asked, 'Where are Father's old clothes? He has just appeared to me dressed in a white shirt, black clothes and felt slippers, and told me that after leaving home he sewed a large roll of bills inside his grey shirt with a piece of my red dress, and the money is still there.'

The family believed that she was hallucinating, but to set her mind at rest they retrieved the clothes. They found them to be exactly as the girl had described. A roll of notes was sewn into the shirt with a piece of red cloth of the same material as the daughter's dress.

The SPR investigated numerous mediums, testing their communication for accuracy and carefully weighing up the evidence they produced. They were fortunate in having some excellent mediums to work with, one of the most famous being the American, Mrs Leonora Piper.

Mrs Piper had already made a profound impression upon several members of the society, including William James, the psychologist, who was one of the founders of the American SPR and the world-famous physicist, Sir Oliver Lodge, when the investigation was taken over by the sceptical Richard Hodgson of the American SPR. Hodgson had an acquaintance, George Pellew, who had been killed in a riding accident in 1892. Hodgson took some 150 sitters to Mrs Piper, all of whom had known Pellew when he was alive. Through Mrs Piper, Pellew identified each one of them correctly and showed a close knowledge of their affairs. Never once did he mistake a stranger for a friend.

One of the sitters showed him a stud he was wearing. Pellew immediately said through Mrs Piper, 'That's mine. My mother gave it to you', a statement the sitter denied but was later found to be true. Though a reluctant believer, Hodgson was forced to concede that his dead friend was really speaking to him through the entranced medium.

The importance of the SPR's contribution to psychical research cannot be overestimated. Though today it focuses its attention mainly on ESP, its archives are a fascinating mine of information for any serious investigator. It should not be thought, however, that the society consists entirely of believers. Some of its members are arch-sceptics and will rigorously examine every case in an endeavour to find some alternative explanation rather than accepting the spirit hypothesis. Infuriating though this approach is to those who consider that the case for life after death has been proved many times over, it does at least mean that whatever evidence is published by the society cannot be dismissed lightly.

Drop-in Communicators

A particularly interesting type of phenomenon, and one which features in the SPR's records, is that of drop-in communicators. These, as the name implies, are spirit communicators unknown to the sitters who drop in unexpectedly. They seem to have no connection with the sitters and no obvious motive for coming. Sometimes they give information about themselves which can later be checked. One such case was investigated by Dr Alan Gauld of the SPR and published by him in his book *Mediumship and Survival*.

In the 1940s a group of people in Cambridge held sessions over a number of years and kept careful notes of what transpired. Most of the communicators were relatives and friends of the sitters, but there were a number of 'drop-in' communicators as well. One of these gave his name as Harry Stockbridge and volunteered the following information about himself:

> Second Loot attached Northumberland Fusiliers.
> Died Fourteen July Sixteen.
> Tyneside Scottish.
> Tall, dark, thin. Special features large brown eyes.
> I hung out in Leicester . . . Leicester hold[s] a record.
> [Asked what were his likes and dislikes] Problems any.
> Pepys reading.
> Water colouring.
> [Asking if he knew a 'Powis Street' about which two sitters had dreamed]
> I know it well. My association took my memory there.
> [Asked if his mother was with him] Yes.

The sitters did not try to check out this information, but some years later Dr Gauld decided to see if he could trace the unseen visitor. Searching army records, he found that a Second Lieutenant H. Stockbridge of the Northumberland Fusiliers was killed on 14 July 1916. (The records gave the date as 19 July but the death certificate, which Dr Gauld also located, verified 14 July as the correct date.) Before his death Stockbridge had been transferred to a Tyneside Scottish battalion.

The statement 'Leicester holds a record' proved harder to pin down as Stockbridge's name was not on the war memorial at Leicester. It was, however, on a war memorial in his old school in Leicester. It was also established that there was a Powis Street near where he was born.

Dr Gauld traced Stockbridge's surviving relatives who confirmed the details of his appearance and the fact that his mother was dead at the time of the communication. It was not possible to establish whether he had been interested in reading Pepys and water colouring, but the statement that he enjoyed solving problems was indicated by the fact that he had won prizes at school for mathematics and physics.

No one in the Cambridge circle had access to this information, which Dr Gauld only located after considerable time and effort. Nor would the circle have had any reason to concoct such a story since they never sought publicity or made the record of their sittings public.

The traditional ghostly apparition can provide startling evidence. Of course, some apparitions can be put down to hallucination, but this explanation is harder to accept in cases where the spirit form is seen by more than one person, passes on some information unknown to the person who sees it or if it leaves something tangible behind. Psychiatrist Dr Elisabeth Kübler-Ross recounts in her book *On Life After Death* how she was visited by the spirit of one of her former patients.

The incident occurred at a difficult time in her life, when she was dissatisfied with the seminars on dying which she was conducting and was thinking of giving up her work at the University of Chicago. She was standing with a colleague waiting for the lift, when she saw standing in front of her a woman she recognised. It was one of her patients who had died ten months before. The moment the colleague had entered the lift the woman spoke, asking if she could walk with Dr Ross to her office. Dr Ross agreed and walked along beside her, wondering all the while if this was really happening. When they reached the office the woman said:

'Dr Ross, I had to come back for two reasons. One, to thank you and Reverend Gaines . . .' (He was a beautiful black minister with whom I had a super, ideal symbiosis) 'to thank you and him for what you did for me. But the other reason I had to come back is that you cannot stop this work on death and dying, not yet.'

I looked at her, and I don't know if I thought by then, 'It could be Mrs Schwarz,' I mean, this woman had been buried for ten months, and I didn't believe in all that stuff. I finally got to my desk. I touched everything that was real. I touched my pen, my desk, my chair, and it's real. I was hoping that she would disappear. But she didn't. She just stood there and stubbornly, but lovingly, said, 'Dr Ross, do you hear me? Your work is not finished. We will help you, and you will know when the time is right, but do not stop now. Promise?'

I thought, 'My God, nobody would ever believe me if I told them this, not even my dearest friend.' Little did I know I would later tell this to several hundred people. Then the scientist in me won, and I said something very shrewd and a big fat lie. I said to her, 'You know Reverend Gaines is in Urbana now.' (This was true; he had taken over a church there.) I said, 'He would just love to have a note from you. Would you mind?' And I gave her a piece of paper and a pencil. You understand, I had no intention of sending this note to my friend, but I needed scientific proof. I mean, somebody who's buried can't write little love letters. And this woman, with the most human, no, not human, most loving smile, knowing every thought I had – and I knew, it was thought transference if I've ever experienced it – took the paper and wrote a note. Then she said (but without words), 'Are you satisfied now?' I looked at her and thought, I will never be able to share this with anybody, but I am going to really hold onto this. Then she got up, ready to leave, repeating: 'Dr Ross, you promise,' implying not to give up this work yet. I said, 'I promise.' And the moment I said, 'I promise,' she disappeared.

   We still have the note.

One of the finest mediums of modern times was Estelle Roberts. In a career spanning half a century (she died in 1970) she gave comfort to hundreds of people and was particularly well known for the public demonstrations of clairvoyance she gave at the Royal Albert Hall and the Queen's Hall in London. Mrs Roberts was held in great respect by all who knew her.

   Mrs Margaret Wagstaff of Surrey told me about a series of sittings she had with her in the 1950s. Mrs Wagstaff's father, Sir John Marshall, who had been director of India's Archeological Department, had become an invalid which made him so depressed that he felt life was no longer worth living. In an effort to help him, she suggested that she

should seek, on his behalf, to obtain proof of survival
through a medium. Her father agreed, on condition that she
went to the best medium in England who, at that time, was
Estelle Roberts.

At the first sitting Estelle began by saying:

'There are a lot of people here, wanting to come
through.' She then *named* George, Hugo, Will,
Annie, Henry and others, all from my father's loving
family – some of whom I had never met, nor indeed
had I ever had any interest in the older members of
that generation.

'Give my loving greetings to Jack and Florrie on
their anniversary today,' said Will. When I read the
record of that session to my parents, Jack and
Florrie, called by those names in the family, *none* of
us could think of a birthday anniversary that day.
But suddenly my father said: 'Oh, it's our wedding
anniversary today.'

Reminded of their wedding anniversary by my
father's brother, Will, we were also reminded that,
when on earth, Will was the one and only member of
that large family who always remembered birthdays
and other anniversaries and frequently wrote a poem
to celebrate the event.

Lord Curzon, Viceroy of India, was a great friend of Mrs
Wagstaff's father and encouraged him in his work. Some of
the messages were from him:

Estelle: 'Greetings from Curzon to your father. He
wants your father to know that he has met one of the
great masters of India – Mahamo . . . a twelve letter
word. He is interested in your father's spiritual
welfare.'

When Mrs Wagstaff read out the message to her father he identified the name at once as Mahamogalana, one of the Buddha's disciples, whose stupa (shrine) Sir John had helped to restore. On another occasion, Lord Curzon reminded Sir John of an incident that had occurred many years before:

> He asked my father to 'remember the *two* elephants'. This, of course, made no sense to me, but when I read that message to my father he said, 'Of *course* I remember. Curzon and I were standing in front of two great stone elephants and I slipped and fell against Curzon's back, giving him a lot of pain as he suffered from a bad back over a long period. You can imagine how bad I felt about that incident.'

These sittings, she says, changed her father's outlook, replacing depression with hope and loving expectation.

The idea that the dead can make phone calls may seem too far-fetched to believe, but there are a number of strange cases on record collected by D. Scott Rogo and other well-known researchers into the paranormal. An intriguing story which is told in Scott Rogo's book *Life After Death* was recounted to him by a Hollywood actress who asked him not to reveal her identity.

When Miss Adams, as he calls her, was eight years old, she and her family were having a Thanksgiving get-together at the home of a family friend. Two years previously, the friend's daughter, who had always returned home for Thanksgiving, had been killed in a car accident. When the phone rang, Miss Adams answered it:

> I . . . heard the long-distance operator say, 'I have a collect call.' She mentioned the name of my mother's friend and she mentioned the name of the daughter.

[In other words, the call was addressed to the friend, and the operator told Miss Adams that the call was from the deceased daughter.] This threw me a little bit even as a child, and I said, 'Just a minute.' I went and got my mother's friend. She came to the phone. I stood watching her because I had heard the name and thought that maybe somebody was playing a joke on me or her or something. She listened on the phone, turned absolutely white, and fainted.

Later on I heard what happened. There was a great hushing up about it, but I learned that she had heard her daughter – who had been dead two or three years – speak to her. She said the same thing she always did before she came home; 'Mommie, it's me,' she said. 'I need twenty dollars to get home.'

The mother always sent her twenty dollars for good luck. She said she recognized the voice. They called the phone company, but they had no record of any phone call.

In a few instances information from beyond the grave has been instrumental in solving crimes. In 1979 in Illinois, USA a Filipino nurse, Teresita Basa, was stabbed to death in her apartment from which her jewellery was stolen. The police had no suspects and it seemed that the murder would remain unsolved but a friend of the murdered woman, Remy Chura, began having repeated dreams in which Teresita told her that she had been murdered by a man called Allan Showery, who had given her jewellery to his girlfriend, whom she also named. After some hesitation Remy Chura went to the police with her story. The police questioned Showery and when they raided his home and that of his girlfriend they found Teresita's jewellery. He was tried and found guilty of Teresita's murder.

Sittings with mediums are sometimes disappointing. In

some cases the standard of work leaves a lot to be desired
and the information offered is so vague that it could apply
to anyone. However, there are some excellent mediums
around who produce evidence that challenges even the most
determined sceptic to come up with any explanation other
than the obvious one – that spirit communication can and
does take place.

It is difficult to convey on paper the impact of a good
sitting. A proficient medium will not only give correct facts
about a communicator but will also convey their character
in a way that might mean little to an outsider but which to
the recipient is utterly convincing. Margaret Rose from Mer-
seyside told me of a sitting she had with the Enfield
medium, Tom Flynn, from which I will quote just a short
part.

Margaret's husband Tony died in 1993. She had always
been a believer in life after death and was conscious that
Tony was still around her but she hadn't felt the need to
consult a medium. But one day last year a friend who had
had an excellent sitting with Tom made an appointment for
Margaret to go and see him. Unfortunately, at the last
minute she was unable to go but, not to be defeated, Tom
gave her the sitting over the phone.

> Tom described my husband exactly and gave me his
> name. He said, quite accurately, that he had had
> pains all over his body for a few days before his death
> but that he had gone peacefully at the end, while I
> was sitting beside him holding his right hand. Tom
> spoke of daffodils. Tony loved spring flowers and we
> had grown a new variety of daffodils the spring
> before he died, which we had been very proud of. He
> also said that Tony had a mania for shoes, which was
> true, and that he loved wristwatches and paintings.
> He said, 'He knows that you've moved and he

loves the windows!' Then he spoke of a golf course
and asked if Tony played golf. After Tony died I
moved to a new flat in an old building which has
particularly attractive and unusual windows – and it
overlooks the golf course.

There were other personal details, including a message that
went straight to Margaret's heart – 'Tell her she was the only
one I ever really loved.' This was something Tony had said
to her many times.

'I was apprehensive about speaking to Tom,' Margaret
admitted, 'but he was gentle and put me at my ease. The
sitting brought me such comfort.'

I have had many sittings over the years. It might be
thought that, as a medium myself, I shouldn't find this necessary, but it's always interesting to receive contact with loved
ones through a person who doesn't know me or them, and it
gives my spirit people a chance to say things that, for whatever reason, they can't say to me direct.

One of the best sittings I had was with the well-known
London medium, Ronald Hearn, It was all the more impres-
sive because I wasn't actually present at the time. I wrote to
Mr Hearn asking if he could make contact with my uncle
who had died recently, though I added that I realised it is
not always possible to reach a particular person and that I
would be happy to hear whatever the spirit world had to say
to me. My uncle, however, heard my request. A couple of
weeks later, back came a tape recording from Mr Hearn.

It left me in no doubt that my uncle had come through
to him. Ron's description was very exact: a very interesting
man, always dressed smartly when he went out in public, an
engaging smile and a dry sense of humour, 'as honest as the
day is long'. To recount the whole sitting would take too
long but I will just give a few short extracts and my
comments:

Something unusual about his hair. He had a good head of pure white hair.

Clever with his hands. He was a builder and was always doing work in his home.

Did he have problems with his chest? He suffered from leukaemia but developed a chest infection a few days before he died.

Would the name of Harry have any connection? This was his name.

Something to do with an antique mahogany cabinet . . . lots of pictures. He collected antique furniture and pictures.

An old clock . . . it could be a grandfather clock. He left me a grandfather clock.

A rectangular table. He says. 'It's a pity about the table.' He had an old table which was damaged and which I had to have repaired.

A lot of cars . . . was he very interested in cars? He had a number of classic cars during the course of his life which were his pride and joy.

I get the smell of strong cheese. His love of strong-smelling cheese was a joke in the family.

I see a couple of cameras. After his passing you found a couple of cameras and wondered, what did he have these for? I found some cameras when clearing out his house after he died and wondered where he got them.

He gives me the impression of an enormous bouquet of flowers, beautifully arranged. There was an enormous bouquet of flowers on his coffin which I took home and arranged.

I don't need an ear trumpet now! He was very deaf prior to his passing.

A very special book, beautifully bound. It may be in the family. The family photograph album, which I have now.

I hear beautiful organ music. Did he play the organ? No, but I do, and I am often conscious of him there when I am playing in church.

The whole tape gave me a strong sense of my uncle's personality, and of the love and support he was bringing me from the spirit world. Truly, death does not divide.

Establishing Contact For Yourself

These are just a few stories chosen to illustrate the range and strength of the case for life after death. I could give many more but, in the end, the belief in survival is a very personal matter. For many people, it's not enough to read about it or hear of the experiences of others. They need to make their own search and establish contact for themselves with someone known to them in the spirit world.

So where do you begin? The easiest way is to visit your local spiritualist church. The address should be in the phone book. If not, the Spiritualist National Union or the Greater World Christian Spiritualist Association should be able to tell you where your nearest church is. A number of churches advertise in *Psychic News*. The addresses of all these organisations are given at the back of this book.

Don't be put off by the word 'church'. The services are very informal and not at all stuffy. All services include a short demonstration of clairvoyance. If you're not one for hymn singing, most churches also put on demonstrations which are not in the context of a religious service.

Attend the church regularly if you can. Churches try to vary their mediums as much as possible so you will probably see a different one every time, and you will find that their style, as well as their standard, varies enormously.

It will also be helpful to you to mix with like-minded people who don't think you're strange for wanting to 'talk to the dead'.

The church will be able to recommend a medium with whom you can have a private sitting. This is a more satisfactory way of trying to obtain evidence because the conditions are better; you have time and privacy. Try to approach the sitting with an open mind. For communication to be successful, a very delicate balance needs to be established between the medium, the sitter and the communicators. If you are nervous or over-emotional because of a recent bereavement you may unconsciously be disrupting this balance and setting up a barrier. Remember also that your spirit people may find it hard to get through to you – it is their first visit to a medium too!

Don't fix your mind upon any one person in the hope of hearing from them. Generally, if there is a strong link of love with a particular person, it is possible to establish communication but this is not always the case. They may not be there, or the medium may be unable to connect with them. You may get casual acquaintances from years back or relatives who died before you were born. In most cases, they are drawn to you because they feel an affinity with you, for reasons best known to themselves, though I suspect that a few of them come for the same reason that people on earth go to mediums – out of curiosity to see what happens!

In assessing the value of a sitting, you need to make allowances for the difficulties of communication. By its nature, things can never be cut and dried. There are bound to be some errors and misinterpretations but, taken as a whole, it should be meaningful to you. Use your own intuition and common sense to judge whether what you are told rings true. Did you feel helped and comforted by it? One of the hallmarks of a good sitting is that it should have given you hope and encouragement, and possibly some helpful insights into yourself and your life.

You may need to have several sittings before you are able to say, hand on heart, that you truly believe in spirit communication. With many people conviction builds up slowly over a period of time. This was the case for me when my father died. I had a number of sittings following his death and also attended my local spiritualist church. Time after time, mediums who knew nothing about me or my family would describe him to me, giving details which, in some cases, were known only to the two of us. One of them told me that he was with someone called Joe, which meant nothing to me at the time. Only months later did I learn that Joe was his father's name. Perseverance is the key to success, as in so many other things. There are very few people who have searched in sincerity and have failed to find the conviction they were seeking. Those people who reject life after death out of hand are usually the ones who have never bothered to look at the evidence.

It's a good idea to make notes of all sittings or to tape record them if the medium has no objection to this. Sometimes things that mean nothing at the time can prove very significant later on. If you are given any information about deceased relatives that you don't know about, try to check it out with other members of the family. If it proves correct, this will be very good evidence for you. And be patient. All the while you are searching you are building up your knowledge of the spirit world. You are also, whether you are aware of it or not, enhancing your own psychic awareness.

This psychic awareness is something that is inborn in all of us. Developing it is not so much a matter of acquiring a new skill, more a matter of getting in touch with our inner selves and unfolding a latent natural ability. In the next section of the book I will be showing how you can do this and how you can gain your own, inner conviction that death is not the end.

PART II

Developing Your Ability As A Medium

7

THE RAINBOW
BRIDGE

In the first half of this book we looked at how closely the two worlds are interwoven, and how naturally contact takes place between ourselves and those in spirit. I described how you can start to become aware of the spiritual dimension, building your contact with your own loved ones. Now we are going to take this further and see how the gift of mediumship is developed. I will be covering all aspects of this, from communication with the astral plane (what is generally known as clairvoyance), to trance and channelling through which we can link with still higher dimensions. Mediumship can operate on many different levels and it is part of a medium's skill to understand these levels and know which one they are working on.

'Why should anyone want to be a medium?' I was once asked during an interview on BBC Radio Scotland. 'Why do you want to talk to dead people?'

I must admit to being somewhat taken aback at what seemed to me a very silly question. The first answer that sprang to mind was that they're not dead otherwise I couldn't talk to them! The second was that it brings great comfort to the bereaved to know that those they love are still with them. But mediumship does more than this. By demonstrating that there is a world beyond and by obtaining knowledge of what that world is like it removes the fear of death. It also enriches this life because it shows that we are more than a physical body that perishes. We are immortal beings containing a spark of divinity and each of us has a part to play in the shaping of the universe.

A few years ago it was fairly unusual to find anyone who would openly admit to believing in life after death. When I began working as a medium I had to contend with being treated as something of an oddity. The last few years have, however, seen a remarkable shift in public opinion. Now, though of course I encounter many people who are not convinced one way or the other, it isn't often that I come across anyone who dismisses the subject out of hand. The majority of people are at least prepared to keep an open mind. And a lot of them, given a little gentle encouragement, will tell me stories of psychic experiences they have had. So my sceptical interviewer friend was somewhat out of touch in thinking that 'talking to dead people' is something weird or bizarre. As the examples already given demonstrate, a great many people have had contact with the spirit world, one way or another.

Some of these people want to go on and deepen that contact by becoming mediums themselves but they don't know how to go about it. They imagine that it is a rare gift, bestowed only on a few privileged individuals. Fortunately, this is not the case. Mediums of outstanding calibre, like geniuses in any field, are rare and as a rule show their talents unmistakably in childhood. But most people who are at all sensitive can cultivate some degree of awareness of the spirit world.

Inherited Ability

It helps if you were born into a psychic family since the ability is often inherited. Some of the strongest mediums I know had parents who were similarly gifted, although in some cases they rebelled against it as teenagers and only returned to the fold in later life. Having parents who are sensitive helps in other ways. Many children are naturally aware of the spirit world. If they grow up in a sympathetic environment their awareness flowers, but if they are discouraged from speaking about it or, even worse, told off for 'making up stories' they learn to suppress their gifts. They may do this so effectively that if they want to develop them as adults they find it difficult because they have a lot of deep-seated fear and resistance to overcome.

Having spoken to a great many mediums, I would say that the vast majority were sensitive as children. It is rare for mediumship to develop suddenly in a person who has never had psychic experiences of any kind. I have come across mediums who have assured me that their gifts arrived 'out of the blue' with no warning, but I find this hard to believe. For a person to be a successful medium there must be some degree of inborn awareness and an instinctive link with the spirit world, however slight. To this extent mediums have to be born rather than made, though even a slight awareness can be cultivated.

What does happen in many cases is that a crisis or trauma in a person's life will cause the dormant ability to manifest for the first time. Many mediums discover their gift when they lose someone close to them. In reaching out to that person they awaken their capacity for mediumship and, having done so, they then go on to use it for the benefit of others.

The trauma does not have to be a bereavement. Illness or a period of intense stress or anxiety can have a similar effect. I find this to be the case with many young mediums. They have not known the pain of losing anyone dear to them but they have suffered in some way, perhaps through unemployment, or the break-up of a marriage or relationship, something that has turned their life upside down and made them reassess what is important to them and where they are going.

It seems to me that, when we are absorbed in the material world and everything is going well we ignore our inner being as if we had built a wall around it. It is only when something dramatic or tragic breaks down that wall that the softer, gentler, intuitive side of our nature emerges. It is a sad truth that the greatest lessons that we learn in this life are learned through suffering. Yet often it is possible to look back on such times and see that they have led us to fulfil ourselves in ways we would never have dreamed of.

The Vocation Of Mediumship

Some mediums drift into their work without any conscious planning. They are invited to sit in a development group and accept, thinking it might be an interesting thing to do for a while and that they can give it up if they get bored with it. Of course, there are people who decide it's not for them and leave, but others become drawn in and find, rather to their own surprise, that they are more gifted than they thought they were. You may think that you've chosen to be a medium but in fact the spirit world has chosen you. You may have made the choice before you were born. Possibly you were trained as a psychic or a seer in a former life. Your guides were probably with you before birth and will have been watching over you ever since, waiting for the appropriate time for you to enter on to this pathway.

But, however you begin, once you elect to become a medium it is a life-long commitment. You may at times want to give it up but you will always be drawn back, very lovingly but firmly. The spirit world is subtle in its methods. There have been many times when I have been disheartened and have threatened to give up the whole thing, then someone I couldn't refuse would ask for a sitting or a church service would go really well. Suddenly my enthusiasm would come flooding back and I would know that there was nothing else I wanted to do.

For mediumship is a vocation. Just as people go to the doctor for help when they are ill, so at times of trouble or bereavement they may turn to a medium to comfort them. You owe it to them to give your service in sincerity. Of course, no medium can be 100 per cent accurate or give a successful sitting every single time, but it is your responsibility to make yourself as fine an instrument as you can to link the two worlds together.

Meditation

The purpose of meditation

So, if you want to become a medium and you think you have the potential, how do you go about it? The first thing, even before you start sitting in a development circle, is to learn to meditate. These days, meditation is very popular and is used for a variety of purposes. Some people use it as a therapy to help them cope with the stresses and strains of life. Others see it as a means of self-healing or a way of seeking enlightenment. It is of great value in all these ways, but for mediumship it is essential.

Firstly and most obviously, you must learn to still the outer mind and raise your level of consciousness if you are to attune to the finer vibrations of the spirit world. The more still and receptive your mind, the more accurately you will be able to receive what is transmitted to you. Secondly, meditation will put you in touch with your inner self. It will give you a source of strength and, believe me, you are going to need it. It will also give you stability, and the ability to distinguish between your own mind and what is coming from the spirit.

More than that, it will give you wisdom. There is infinite wisdom within each one of us, if we can reach deeply enough inside ourselves to find the source. One of your tasks as a medium is to be a teacher. This does not only mean passing on teaching from spirit. You teach by what you are and by the way you live your life.

Lastly, but most importantly, meditation links you with the light of God and the spirit world. It doesn't matter whether you are a spiritualist, or follow another church religion or philosophy, since all true religion is based on love and service. If you want to communicate with the spiritual dimension then you must yourself become spiritual. Of course, the astral realm consists of many different dimensions, and some of these are far from being evolved, but as a medium you intend (I hope!) to connect with beings of light so you must raise yourself to that level. Remember that like attracts like. The higher you can lift your thoughts, the more beautiful and the more evolved will be the beings you will draw to help you and work with you.

Meditation need not be difficult. You do not need to spend hours contemplating your navel or tie yourself up in knots performing all sorts of elaborate postures. A few minutes every day, or perhaps twice a day, will suffice. If you persevere you will find that it becomes an integral part of your life – in fact, after a little while you will wonder how you ever managed without it.

A spiritual being

Later in this chapter I am going to give you a meditation exercise you can try, which is designed to open your awareness to the spirit world. But before I do that I want to put some ideas to you, to ask you to look at yourself as a spiritual being whose true home is beyond this world.

Quite recently, I was at a meeting of a New Age group. They were a mixed crowd of people, of all ages. During the course of the discussion the group leader asked, 'How many of you believe you have a soul?'

All the hands went up, some more hesitantly than others. Then a woman at the back commented, 'I see it the other way round. I *am* a soul and I *have* a body.'

Some of the group agreed with her. For others, the idea was new. Certainly, it is a concept that turns our usual way of thinking upside down. We identify with the physical body. After all, it is the part of ourselves we are most familiar with. We feed it, clothe it, worry if it is too fat or too thin. But the body is not the real you. The soul within is what matters, not only because that is the part of you that survives death, but also because it is what you really are, here and now.

The New Age writer and philosopher, Sir George Trevelyan, wrote in his book *Exploration into God*:

> The body can be seen as the wonderfully designed
> temple in which this divine being can operate while
> living through its present life-span in the heavy
> density of matter. The body can of course die and be
> dissolved, but that only releases the eternal soul-
> entity back into the spirit world from which it came.

Thus in our death-ridden culture we can grasp that
for this being, this 'I', *there simply is no death.*
Survival is axiomatic. But more important is the
concept of pre-existence. You were there as a
developed soul before you were born. Planet Earth
can be seen as the training ground for souls in long
evolution through the Fall and back to God.

This passage raises a number of interesting points. Firstly,
what do we mean by 'soul'? We speak of the soul as the
essence of a thing. We even say that a gregarious person is
the 'life and soul of the party'. Perhaps the simplest way
of putting it is to describe the soul as our inner being. It is
not something which is created at birth. When a child is
born, the soul is already there. Opinions differ as to precisely
when between conception and birth, the soul enters the
foetus; perhaps it varies from person to person, depending
on the soul's eagerness or reluctance to embark on a new
life.

Hidden within the soul are deep memories; memories
of its former lives on earth and the intervals in between
spent in the spirit world. At a conscious level we remember
none of these. The ancients believed that souls re-entering
the earth had to drink of the Lethe, the River of Forgetful-
ness. But the recollections remain locked in the subconscious. Occasionally they may surface in dreams or in
meditation, when we may picture ourselves living in a
former time. If we feel drawn to a particular time or culture
it may be because we were on earth at the time or in that
place.

Memories can also surface under hypnosis, using a technique called past-life regression. This can be a very valuable
therapeutic tool. Our present personalities are the sum total
of all our past lives and experiences. By tapping into these
hidden memories we can learn to understand ourselves

better. Some of our fears and phobias have their origin in past lives. For instance, a person who has an irrational fear of drowning may have drowned in a former incarnation. If we are strongly drawn to a stranger we meet it may be that we knew and loved them in a past life. The soul remembers and recognises them. Many of the people who shape our present lives, our families, friends and loved ones, will all be acquaintances from the past.

Young children, because they are still close to the spirit world, may spontaneously recall memories. These are usually dismissed by adults as fantasies. As the child becomes absorbed in its new life these memories quickly fade. The child's personality develops, shaped partly by heredity, and partly by its upbringing and environment. But the pre-existent soul forms the bedrock of that personality.

So, let us go back a stage further and ask, where did this soul come from in the first place? According to ancient spiritual teaching, we were created by God, drops of water from the Ocean of Eternity. God put a small part of himself into everything he created. This eternal, unchanging part of ourselves is our spirit. It goes under many names: the Jewel in the Lotus; the Pearl of Great Price; the Divine Spark.

The words 'soul' and 'spirit' are often used interchangeably, but they are not the same thing. The soul forms a vehicle, or outer clothing for the spirit, in much the same way that the physical body forms an outer clothing for the soul while we are on earth. The soul dwelt originally close to God, in a state of innocence. But in order to mature it had to move away from God, as a child has to move away from its parents if it is to grow up. So our souls began the long journey of evolution, descending gradually, in aeons of time, through the various planes of the spirit world until they reach the astral.

But even this, though it was far removed from their

place of origin, did not provide sufficient challenges for all they needed to learn. So they came into physical incarnation, taking residence in bodies of flesh. This physical world was – and is – the hardest part of the soul's journey. The earth is the darkest, most dense of the planes. It is the soul's battlefield, where it has to undergo suffering, poverty, disease and all the hardships which do not exist in any other dimension. We come here many times and will continue to come back until we have learned all the lessons earth has to teach us. But between each life – and the time between is usually much longer than the period spent here – we stay in the spirit world, which is where we truly belong.

This may be the origin of the legend of the Fall. According to the Bible, Adam and Eve were thrown out of the Garden of Eden because they dared to eat of the Tree of Life. It is possible to see this story as an allegory of human descent from the spirit world on to the earth. Viewed in this way, the Fall was a fall forward, a necessary step, since humankind could not mature spiritually until they had experienced life on the physical plane and learned to overcome evil with good.

All over the world, there are legends of a Golden Age, a state of paradise when people walked with the gods and lived in peace and harmony with nature. This, too, for legends are woven of many strands, may be a memory, deeply buried in the subconscious, of the paradise condition of the astral world which humankind had to leave behind.

The idea of death as a home-coming is beautifully expressed in the following spirit communication given in *The Country Beyond* by Jane Sherwood.

Here is our home, here our native air, obtained at last
at the cost of who knows what of struggle, suffering
and sinning, repenting, expiating and accepting. At

last we are at home – in the Father's mansions,
even if as yet, we may not come into His presence. I
think I understand now what is the deep hunger and
desire which assails us in all experiences of beauty. It
is the nostalgia for home, for the never quite
forgotten bliss we have had to leave. It is the pain of
comparing the earthly with the unfading knowledge
of the heavenly. I doubt whether the most evil, lost
and wandering soul ever loses this hunger of desire,
and sooner or later it must bring him back up the
steep ascent and into the Fatherland.

The sense of nostalgia is something that many people can
identify with. It is felt more strongly in childhood, though
the child does not have the words to express it. Many
mediums, healers and sensitive people I have spoken to have
confided to me that, as children, they didn't feel at home in
the world. They felt different, set apart. One said to me, 'I
felt I was a stranger in a strange land.'

I believe this is one reason why a person is born with
the gift of mediumship. They are aware of the spirit world
because, at a deep level, they have never lost touch with it.
To be attuned to the spirit is natural to them. Those they
know as guides and helpers are companions they knew and
loved before they came here, who have undertaken to guide
them through their earthly journey.

I do not mean to be depressing, or to give the impression that we should spend our lives waiting to enter the
astral world, even if it is happier than this one. I enjoy my
life here and believe in living it to the full. Despite its harsh-
ness and ugliness, this is still a beautiful world and it needs,
as never before in history, spiritually minded men and
women to look after it and save humankind from havoc. But
it does put everything in a different perspective if we look at
this life as just one of many, a small step along our eternal

journey. And it helps to know that, whatever happens to us, however difficult or painful it may be, nothing can destroy the soul within or cut us off completely from our spiritual origins.

For that awareness of the spiritual world is something we carry with us. It only waits to be rediscovered. The myths of the Golden Age speak of the time when heaven and earth were linked by a rainbow bridge of many colours, across which souls could pass. When the Golden Age ended, humankind lost contact with the heavenly state and the rainbow bridge was closed. Only priests, shamen and holy people could cross it to meet those dwelling on the other side. But the rainbow bridge still exists. It is our link with the world of spirit, and it is also our link with our own spiritual selves. And meditation is the way to find it.

Preparing to meditate

If you have never meditated before, it is best to start slowly. A few minutes a day is enough at first. Later you may try extending it to half an hour or more, depending upon how much time you have available.

But before you even begin, try to prepare the mind. If you are stressed, anxious or over-tired when you sit down to meditate, you cannot hope to achieve much. Later, if you have made it a regular habit, you will find that the very act of sitting down in your accustomed chair and closing your eyes will have a calming effect but, in the early stages, you may find yourself easily distracted.

A good way of preparing yourself is to go for a walk in the country or, if this is not possible, in the park. Feel your closeness to nature and let yourself be moved by its beauty. We are all part of the universe. Each living thing, each bird, each tree, each blade of grass is part of God's creation and has a spark of his divine life within it. Touch the petals of the flowers and feel their softness. Sense the powerful energy that radiates from the trees – try leaning against the trunk of a sturdy old tree and feeling its strength flow into you. Breathe in the warmth of the sun and know you are taking in not just the physical heat but the energy of life itself.

If it's a dreary, overcast day or pouring with rain, none of this may sound like a very good idea. In that case, you might try listening to beautiful music or reading a book that you find inspiring. The idea is to lift your mind above your everyday cares and worries so that your consciousness can rise to a higher level.

If you can set aside one room of your house as a place of meditation, that is ideal, but if space does not permit this, choose a quiet corner somewhere and make it your own. You might like to put fresh flowers there or hang a picture that makes you feel restful. Incense, joss sticks or aromatherapy oils can be useful to help create a good atmosphere. Many tapes of New Age music are available which provide a good background.

The meditation exercise

▷ Now for the actual meditation exercise. This exercise is designed to take you on a journey that will lead you to the centre of your being. You will need just one piece of equipment – a mirror. It need not be a large one. A handbag mirror will suffice. Choose a time when you will not be disturbed. Unplug the phone or take it off the hook. You might like to dim the light but don't make the room completely dark. Sit in the spot you have chosen. Loosen any tight clothing, relax, and take some deep breaths. Don't hurry, and don't at this stage think of making contact with the world of spirit. For the time being, you are going to concentrate on getting to know yourself.

Now look into the mirror. Concentrate steadily at the face you see. You think you know it so well. You see it every morning when you stand at the bathroom mirror, but how well do you really know the person behind it? Gaze into the eyes. It is said that the eyes are the mirror of the soul. It has also to be said that, if you polish the mirror of your soul, you will see God's face shining in it.

Be aware that the physical form is not the real you. Say to yourself, 'I am not this body.' And go deeper within.

Now think about what you are feeling. Are you happy or sad, calm or anxious? Often our emotions rule us. They are stronger than our reason. We love, we hate, and we believe we cannot stop ourselves. But emotions are transitory. What seemed important at one time is forgotten next year or even next day. Do not criticise or judge yourself, just observe what you are feeling. And know that these intense feelings of passion, fear or anger are just squalls on the surface of the water. Underneath, the ocean is calm.

So take a step backwards. Detach yourself from your emotions. Say to yourself, 'I am not these feelings. I possess them but they do not possess me.' And ask yourself, who is the one who is feeling?

Go deeper again. The mind is like a well. However far you gaze into it, you will never reach the bottom, but go as deep as you can. Let all the restless chatter of the mind die away. Don't try to force your thoughts to be still. It is impossible to make the mind blank. Just sit and observe the thoughts like waiting for a clockwork mechanism to wind down. It may take a long time, but eventually stillness will come. And in that stillness ask yourself, 'Who is thinking these thoughts?' Try to touch that deepest part of yourself and know that inner self is what you truly are.

Now reach out to the spirit world, to those guides who have charge over you. Don't worry about distinguishing individuals at this stage, just know that you are watched over and protected. Send out your love and try to feel the response. This need not come in words or pictures. The knowing in the heart is sufficient. And if you feel that this is the right time for you and if you are sure that mediumship is the path you wish to follow, silently make your own act of dedication. You could use the following or you may prefer to make up your own words:

Divine heavenly Father, accept my service as an instrument of light. Make me a clear channel for those bright ones who walk beside me that we may work together to bring comfort, love and healing to all in need, and prove to the world that there is no death.

Hold these thoughts steady in your mind for a few minutes. When you feel it is enough, give thanks and close down psychically by picturing a cloak of white light folded tightly all around you (for more on this, see the exercise at the end of Chapter 9). Finally, to bring yourself completely back to earth, have something to eat or drink.

Each time you meditate, reaffirm your link with the spirit world. In this way you will be building your own rainbow bridge, making it ever firmer and more secure. You still have a long way to go but you will have taken the first and most important step. Now for the next one. Are you psychic? Your immediate reaction may be to say 'no', but in that case you are probably underestimating yourself.

8

THE BEGINNINGS OF
AWARENESS

Having A 'Sixth Sense'

'I'm not psychic but . . .' How many times have I heard that?
And then the speaker goes on to recount some incident
which shows that they *are* psychic, even if it only comes in
rare flashes.

Being psychic is not the same as being a medium and
this is not a book about developing psychic powers *per se*.
However, if you want to develop your mediumship, then as
well as learning how to meditate and still the mind you will
have to increase your psychic perception before you can
begin to attune to the spirit world.

In this chapter I am going to outline a few exercises you
can try, either alone or with a group of like-minded friends,
that will help you achieve this. These exercises are designed
to lead you on to the development of mediumship. But first
I want to talk a little about what it means to be psychic.
Where do these powers come from and how can we recognise them in ourselves?

You may think that you are not at all psychic but don't
be too sure. The very fact that you have picked up this book
indicates that you have an interest in psychic matters and

that is a start. Being psychic, intuitive or having a 'sixth sense', whatever you like to call it, doesn't mean that you possess some mystic power denied to ordinary mortals. A great many people – I would say, the majority of the population – are psychic to some degree. Psychic abilities are part of the functioning of our inner being or soul and we are all souls within these material bodies. Unfortunately, because many people deny, or are unaware that this soul exists, they don't hear when it is trying to tell them something.

The signs of psychic awareness are very subtle. They are the promptings we receive and generally ignore, to our cost. For instance, you go out on a fine day without an umbrella although something in you is warning you that it's going to rain – and you subsequently get caught in a downpour. Or you lend money to a person who has an honest face though you sense that they are not to be trusted, and you never see them or your money again. 'If only I'd listened!' you reproach yourself. This is your inner self speaking – and you'd save yourself a great deal of trouble if you paid attention to it.

It is the fault of the society we live in that we repress our sixth sense. Science is the god of our age and science has conditioned us to think that there is nothing outside the material, and that anything which seems to go beyond this should be dismissed as superstition or hallucination. Even today, when the existence of extra-sensory powers such as telepathy, clairvoyance and out-of-the-body experiences have been demonstrated over and over again under laboratory conditions, parapsychology is still not taken seriously by scientists, and any scientist who lends this research any support is ridiculed by colleagues and is likely to find their career ruined.

The attitude percolates down to the general public, with the result that most people are wary of admitting to a belief in the supernatural in case they are laughed at. In fact, though, there is nothing supernatural about being psychic. There is really nothing 'supernatural' at all – just natural laws that we don't fully understand yet. And there can be very few people who haven't at some time in their lives, had some sort of psychic experience. This may not be anything dramatic. It may be something very simple, like thinking of a friend you haven't seen for a long time and receiving a phone call from them the same day. 'What a coincidence!' you say. And I am not claiming that coincidences don't happen – but there is usually more than mere chance involved.

Psychic Dreams

Psychic ability often shows itself in dreams. If you keep a record of your dreams over a period of time you may be surprised to find how many of them are prophetic. This is not to say that they come true in every detail, but some of the elements will be there.

You can test this for yourself. You may already be keeping a dream diary. If not, this is a good time to start. Keep a notebook or tape recorder by your bed and record as much of your dreams as you can remember. Check the record carefully for any premonitions. These can take any form. You may dream of something that happens the next day, someone you meet, even a picture in a book or something you see on television. Often they are of very trivial things or a minor event may appear in a highly dramatised form. I once dreamed that the house next door burned down. Next day, the neighbours set fire to their barbeque, resulting in clouds of smoke but no serious damage!

Sensitivity to atmosphere is another sign of psychic awareness. You may walk into a house and immediately know whether it is a sad or a happy place. The impressions you are picking up may emanate from the present occupants or may have been created by those living there in the past. Many sensitive people have a dislike of being in crowds. The energies and thoughts of all the people milling around them are oppressive and disturbing. The more sensitive you become, the more intolerable it is to be in any atmosphere where there is congestion or disharmony.

Whether you are lucky or unlucky as a person is also linked to your degree of sensitivity. Some people have a knack of being in the right place at the right time. Fortune smiles on them. If they back a horse, it comes in first. Others are just the opposite. The horses they back fail to get past the starting post. If a thunderbolt is going to fall out of a clear blue sky it will fall on their house. Our inner selves are wiser than our material minds. Whenever intuition and reason clash, you can be almost sure that intuition will be right and reason wrong. If you are aware of the promptings that come from within and follow them the path of your life will be a lot smoother.

Testing Your Psychic Powers

▷ One simple way to test your psychic powers is to use a pack of playing cards. Spread the cards face down on the table. Make your mind as calm as possible – any tension or strain will set up a mental block. Pick a card at random and see if you can sense what it is.

Don't take too long over this. The first impression that pops into your mind is likely to be the correct one. If you get no impression at all, you can stimulate your mind by asking yourself questions. Do you sense that the card is red or black? Is it a court card?

Is there a lot of printing on it or is it mainly blank? You may get a mental picture; it may be just a 'knowing'. Don't try the exercise too many times in succession. The mind quickly becomes strained and bored, and the concentration wavers. Practice for a few minutes a day. Believe that you can do it and you will – not every time, but often enough to give you encouragement.

The same exercise can be tried using tarot cards. The varied designs on the cards give the subconscious mind strong images to work on. You may find that you pick up some small detail from the design rather than the complete picture. As the tarot is full of symbolism, the symbolic significance of the card may come into your mind. At this stage don't attempt to give readings from the cards or to foretell the future, either for yourself or for anyone else. The tarot requires long and complex study, as well as a highly developed intuitive skill in interpretation. The results could be misleading, or worrying, should you happen to get a spread which seems to warn of misfortune ahead.

Another method of practising is to try to sense the content of any letters you receive without opening them. Hold the envelope lightly between your fingers or press it to your forehead. See if you can 'feel' what the letter is about or get an impression of the personality of the writer. You can do a similar thing with your birthday and Christmas presents – hold the parcel and try to sense what is inside. If you become good at this it will drive your friends and relations mad!

Colour can be a very useful tool in developing psychic ability. Remember that whatever impressions you get are received at a subconscious level first, then filtered through to the conscious, and the subconscious is highly sensitive to colour. Get some brightly coloured squares of paper or cloth and put them into separate envelopes. Obviously, the envelope must be thick enough so you can't see the colour through it. Then hold one of the envelopes and try to sense what colour is inside. You may find that some of the colours, those to which you are naturally drawn, are easier to 'pick up' than others.

Experiments In Telepathy

If you can get together a small group of friends, you might like to try some experiments in telepathy, or mind-to-mind communication. This will stand you in good stead when you come to develop your mediumship. The whole process of communication is one of telepathy between the medium and those in the spirit world so it will be helpful to form an understanding of how telepathy works. It will also dispel once and for all any lingering notions you may have that mediums get all their information telepathically from the mind of the sitter. A few attempts at mind-reading should be enough to convince you that this would in fact be much more difficult than obtaining it by spirit contact!

▷   No doubt you and your group will think of many different experiments you can try, so I will just offer a few suggestions to start you off. Taking your sheets of coloured paper, let one member of the group concentrate on the colour and try to 'send' it to the rest of the group. The person who is 'sending' the colour should try to flood their mind with it. Think of things you associate with that colour. For instance, if the colour is blue, picture a blue sky or blue sea and try to project that idea as well.

Issue each member of the group with a note pad and pencil then, taking it in turns, ask one of the group to draw a picture or geometrical shape and try to transmit it to the others, who should draw what they are receiving. Keep the drawings quite simple. The other members of the group may pick up the general shape even if they do not know what the object is.

Get one member of the group to think of a name. That person should write the name down on their note pad, and repeat it over and over to themselves, silently, of course. See if anyone else can pick up the name.

Simple though these experiments may be, they should produce some interesting results. It will soon become apparent that some members of the group are better at sending images and others at receiving them. The receivers may have the greater potential for mediumship because their minds are more passive and receptive.

Your experiments will also help you to understand some of the difficulties of spirit communication. For instance, I am sure you will have found the last experiment I suggested, the transmitting of names, to be the least successful. The subconscious mind works in images rather than words. Conveying a name, especially an uncommon name with which the recipient is unfamiliar, is very hard. This is why a medium may be unable to give the name of a communicator even though they may give an accurate description of the communicator's appearance or character. Common names with which the medium is familiar will come across more easily, but surnames or foreign names are extremely difficult to pick up.

Sometimes the receiver will pick up not the image transmitted by the sender but something that they associate with it. For instance, if you draw a triangle and your friend to whom you are attempting to send this picture is interested in Egypt they may pick up the impression of a pyramid. Here, too, is a lesson in the problem of mediumship. A spirit communicator may send a thought to the medium which triggers off some strong association in their mind, and causes them to distort the message.

You will also learn the importance of the right mental attitude. You need to make your mind passive in order to receive, but at the same time you must be alert and attentive. It is like tuning a radio very delicately to a remote foreign station where the least deviation of the needle to either side means that you lose the transmission. But you yourself are the radio, and if you are in a disturbed emotional state, or straining too much, tired or unwell, then the reception is bound to be shaky. Try to stay relaxed and enjoy what you are doing without worrying too much about whether or not it is successful.

Psychometry

One of the best ways to increase your psychic ability in preparation for developing mediumship is to practise psychometry. Every object holds impressions of the people who have owned and handled it. Psychometry is the art of 'reading' these impressions. Persuade some of your friends to give you articles to practise on. Jewellery or watches are ideal, since metal retains the impressions better than cloth or plastic. Preferably the articles should not be things which belong to the friends in question if you know them very well, but should belong to someone

known to them, so that you can check the results for
accuracy.

▷   Hold the article in your hand, and focus on the
    thoughts and impressions that come into your mind.
    Try to build up a picture of the person to whom it
    belongs. Again you could ask yourself questions. For
    instance, do you feel that the owner is a man or a
    woman? Are they young or old, happy or sad, fat or
    thin? Don't dwell on any of the questions for too
    long or your imagination will start to interfere.
        What comes into your mind may be no more than
    a series of disjointed mental pictures, but make a
    note of every image, as most, if not all of them will
    relate to the owner of the object. It is as if you were
    tapping into that person's mind and picking up im-
    pressions of things connected with them; people,
    places or events.

It is interesting to experiment with very old objects such as
stones from historic sites, coins or any ancient artefacts you
can get your hands on. With these, the impressions will be
not so much of individuals as of the times with which those
objects were connected.

If the object has belonged to more than one person, the
impressions you pick up will probably be confused. The
most recent owner, or the one with the strongest personality,
is the one you will pick up on most strongly. Don't confuse
psychometry with mediumship. If the article belonged to
someone who has died you may be able to describe the
person, but you should not assume that you are in contact
with them; you are merely 'reading' the article. Some mediums do use psychometry to help them establish a link with
someone in spirit, but this is not a good way of doing it as it
can lead you to think that you are communicating with the

person, when in fact the impressions you are picking up are coming from the article and nothing else.

Learning To See The Aura

Another topic that plays an important role in mediumship is the aura. The aura can be defined as a force field surrounding the human body in a roughly oval shape. It consists of various different stratas or layers which correspond to the etheric, astral and other invisible bodies of which we are composed.

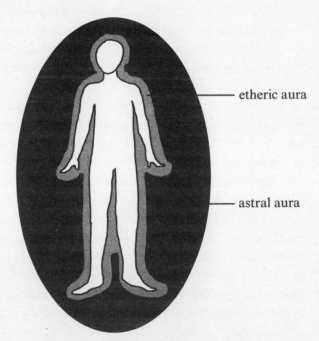

etheric aura

astral aura

The etheric and astral auras

The existence of the aura has to some extent been verified by science. In 1908 Dr Walter Kilner developed a screen consisting of two panes of glass with a coal-tar solution of dicyanin in between, through which he was able to see auras around the patients. After a while the use of the screen sensitised his inner vision so that he was able to see the auras with the naked eye.

A more recent innovation is Kirlian photography. This method, developed about 50 years ago by the Russians, Semyon and Valentian Kirlian, is a means of photographing the energy given off by living objects. Whether these pictures actually capture the aura or some sort of electrical discharge is a matter for scientific debate, but the results indicate that some force is present that transcends the physical.

The Kirlians found, for instance, that if they photographed a leaf that had been cut in half, the missing half of the leaf or its etheric counterpart would appear on the plate. If a healer's hands are photographed while sending out healing, the lines of energy streaming from the finger-tips are stronger and brighter than when the healer is not concentrating the power. And an interesting effect has been noticed with mediums. If a medium wears a wedding ring, when the print has developed there will be a white 'bubble' in the band.

You can find Kirlian machines at many psychic fairs where you can have prints taken of your hands. Also at psychic fairs you will come across an exciting new development; aura vision cameras. This is a new technique that was invented in the USA (where else?) and is now becoming very popular over here. The photos show the aura in colour, though how accurate they are it is difficult to say. Consultants are always on hand to give you an interpretation of what the colours mean.

But whether or not it can be scientifically proved to exist, the aura is something we are all aware of at a subconscious level. This is reflected in our language. We speak of a person being green with envy or feeling 'blue'. We are instinctively attracted to people with whom our auras harmonise and avoid those with whom we clash. Charismatic people have strong auras that extend a long way around them and others are drawn to them, to bask in their energy. Conversely, some individuals are psychic vampires. After a short while in their company you feel exhausted because they have drained the vitality from your etheric field.

Learning to see the aura is a good way of refining your sensitivity. There are various ways in which you can train yourself to do this.

Exercises to help you see auras

▷ Sit in a darkened room and relax. Hold your hands in front of you with the finger-tips touching. Then slowly draw the fingers apart and see if you can see the lines of energy flowing from them.

For the next exercise you will need to enlist the help of a friend. Once again, make the room dim but not completely dark. Get your friend to sit against a dark background. Don't stare at them directly. Look past them, letting your eyes go out of focus. There is a knack to this that is not easy to explain but you'll know when you've got it right.

What you will probably notice first is a whitish-grey mist an inch or two wide that follows the outline of the body. This is the etheric aura. If you are lucky, you may see beyond this various bands of patches of colour. This is the part of the aura that corresponds to the astral body.

To explain the interpretation of these colours requires a book in itself. Should you wish to explore the subject further, I have recommended a book in the Bibliography and Recommended Reading at the end of this book. If you feel discouraged by your apparent lack of progress, it may be reassuring to know that, despite what the books may say, many mediums, including myself, don't see auras at all. But I do sense them, and this can be just as reliable.

▷   You may find that you can sense more easily than you can see. To discover if this is the case, you must once more enlist the assistance of your long-suffering friend. There is no need for a dark room this time. Seat your friend down on a chair and place your hands about a foot above their head. Then slowly bring your hands forward towards the head. At some point, usually 2 or 3 inches away from the body you should detect a slight resistance, like coming up against an invisible barrier. This is the edge of the etheric aura. If your friend is well developed physically or has a lot of vitality, the aura may extend further than this; if they are tired or depleted the auric field will be weak and harder to detect.

Trace the outline of the aura around the body. Do you feel a change in the energy level at any point? Do you sense any particular colour? If you feel a tingling in your fingers, this may indicate a potential for healing.

The ability to sense the aura will help you as a medium to attune to your sitters. It will also enhance your awareness of the astral plane. And then you will be ready to embark on the most important part of your journey – the building of your own rainbow bridge to link you with the world of spirit.

9

SCHOOL FOR
MEDIUMS

The Capacity For Mediumship

You may have visited a spiritualist church or been to a
public demonstration of clairvoyance and wondered how
the medium works. How do they obtain the names and
other information they apparently pluck out of the air? In
the next couple of chapters I am going to explain how it is
done and how the gift is developed. There is no magic for-
mula that can make you into a medium if you don't have the
potential to start with, but there are tried and tested
methods of bringing out your latent ability. If you apply
these, and take the time to work at it seriously, you will be
able to build a bridge of communication with the spirit world
that will enable you to be used as a reliable instrument.

It should be said at the outset that motive is all-
important. It's no good if you want to use your mediumship
as a path to fame and fortune, or if you want to be able to
stand up on a platform and impress people. Nothing less than
total commitment is required. Eileen Roberts, president of
the Institute of Spiritualist Mediums, describes mediumship
as a divine calling: 'Mediums are vehicles for God's work. It's
a sacred gift. A lot of people think they can become mediums

overnight. They don't have the dedication or the training.'

If you feel that you do have that dedication and you are convinced within yourself that this is the path you want to follow, the first thing you will need to know is, do you have the makings of a medium? If you have experimented with some or all of the exercises suggested in the last chapter and have had some degree of success, this indicates that your psychic power is functioning. But do you have the capacity for mediumship? As I have indicated, there is an important difference.

Maybe you have already had some contact with the spirit world of the kind I mentioned earlier, sensing a presence, hearing a voice or just feeling that inner knowing that is so hard to put into words. However brief or slight the contact, all these things indicate that you already have a link with the higher dimension and that is enough to start with. But even if nothing of the kind has happened to you and you still feel drawn to investigate, follow that prompting – it's your own spirit calling you!

I had no exceptional gift as a child. My mother was psychic, though she didn't admit it, and I must have inherited something of this from her. I used to have occasional premonitions and dreams that came true. I also sensed spirit presences, as many children do and heard voices speaking to me inside my head, but these were vague and got mixed up with my own imagination. When I became interested in spiritualism and decided that I would like to be a medium, this was all I had to build on.

Development Circles

Fortunately, I was given a good start. A medium at the church I attended took me under her wing and invited me to join her development circle. This was the beginning of a long process of learning and one that is on-going, because the more you know about spirit communication, the more you realise that we are still just scratching the surface of a vast subject. Now that I teach mediumship myself I am able to pass on what I have learned. I don't claim that my methods are the only way. All I can say is that they work for me, and I hope they will help you too.

The first thing I advise any would-be medium to do is join their local spiritualist church. Mediumship, like measles, is catching. Being in that environment will stimulate your own ability as well as giving you the chance to see how mediums work. The next thing is find a development circle. There may be a circle at your church. If not, a number of organisations such as the College of Psychic Studies and the Spiritualist Association of Great Britain offer training courses (see Useful Addresses at the back of the book).

When you apply to join, you will probably be asked to attend an interview, to assess your suitability and whether you will fit in harmoniously with the other sitters. When I conduct these interviews I am not looking for people who are other-worldly, with their heads stuck in the clouds. I am looking for people who are stable and well balanced, and who have a sincere approach. For your part, you need to make sure the circle is the right one for you. It should be run by a medium you trust and whose work you respect. There is no age limit to joining. It's never too late to learn. However, you should not join unless you are going to be able to attend regularly. Nor should you join a development circle if your health is poor. This includes your mental health. If you suffer from depression or stress, wait until your life is on a more even keel. The process of development will increase your sensitivity and will aggravate any physical or mental condition that may be present.

It is possible to develop mediumship on your own, but

it is far better to do so within a circle. There are several reasons for this. The early stages of development are very confusing, when you are trying to sort out what is real communication and what is the product of your subconscious mind. The circle leader will be able to guide you with this. You will also benefit from the support and encouragement provided by the other members of the group. A group of people sitting together generates a lot of psychic energy and this will stimulate your powers to develop more quickly.

The circle leader should teach you how mediumship works. I say 'should' because the complaint is frequently made to me by those who are sitting in circles that they are not taught this – possibly because the mediums leading them don't understand how it works themselves.

'We just sit there in meditation,' one disgruntled circle member lamented, 'and it's all supposed to happen like magic. Surely there's more to it than that?'

There is a great deal more to it than that. It is true that, by simply meditating and reaching out to the spirit world in thought your mediumship will eventually unfold, but if you understand the mechanics of the process and know how to train your mind you can do a lot to speed things up and also to make your mediumship more reliable.

The essential point to remember is that the spirit world is all around us, but vibrating at a much higher frequency than the physical world. In order to communicate with spirit we have to raise our vibrations, or level of consciousness, so as to bring our minds into harmony with that higher dimension. It is not a matter of 'reaching up' to beings somewhere up in the sky, but rather of 'opening out' our minds, expanding our consciousness so that we can see and hear beyond the range of the physical senses. The purpose of development is to make the mind more sensitive so that it becomes receptive to the spirit world.

A good way of understanding the process is to think of the analogy of the rainbow bridge I mentioned in Chapter 7. Mediums build their half of the bridge by raising their vibrations and attuning to the spirit world. The spirit communicators for their part have to lower their vibrations in order to come within the range of the medium's perception. Hopefully, the two meet somewhere in the middle and the bridge is established across which the communications can pass.

These communications are received telepathically. The spirit communicators create a mental link, impressing thoughts, words and pictures on to the medium's mind. If you have been working on the exercise in telepathy given in Chapter 8, you will realise how hard this is, and will readily appreciate why messages received through mediums are so often vague and unsatisfactory. The communicators can only convey as much as the medium's mind is able to receive. Even this limited amount of information often gets distorted or is so fragmented that it makes little sense. With regular practice the reception becomes clearer but don't expect that you will ever see and hear spirits as if they were flesh and blood. If you could do that, you would be in the spirit world yourself!

There are three different modes of perception: clairvoyance, clairaudience and clairsentience. Clairvoyance, which literally means 'clear seeing', is the ability to see spirit, through in fact it is used as a general term to cover all forms of mediumship as well as the ability to see into the future. Clairaudience is the ability to hear spirit. The voices may sound like external voices but are more often heard inside the head. Music, bells or other sounds may occasionally be heard. Clairsentience is the faculty of sensing spirit. It is the most common mediumistic gift though it is often not recognised as such. If you sense a presence round you or detect something pleasant in the atmosphere of a room or building, you are being clairsentient. Mediums use one or all of these abilities simultaneously.

Later, I will be giving exercises to develop these different modes of perception but first I want to explain another important aspect of mediumship, the psychic centres.

Psychic Centres

There are seven major psychic centres. They are situated in the etheric body in a line corresponding to the spine. Each has a different function and operates on a different level of vibration, from the lowest to the highest. Together they regulate the flow of physical and psychic energy within the body, and provide the link between our material selves and the higher dimensions. As a person develops psychically and spiritually the centres are activated in turn.

The centres are sometimes called 'chakras' from the Sanskrit word for wheel, since they appear in the aura like pulsating wheels of colour. A complete study of this subject would require several chapters, and I have recommended a book in the Bibliography and Recommended Reading, but here I am just going to consider the centres as they relate to mediumship.

The root chakra is located at the base of the spine. This is the centre through which we draw the physical energy necessary for life. In people who are full of vitality, this centre is fully opened or activated. If the centre is blocked or damaged, through injury or perhaps childhood trauma, the person's vitality will be low. A little above this is the sacral centre. This governs sexuality and the instincts. In some systems the second chakra is given as the spleen. This acts as a filter for the psychic energy, and is concerned in astral projection and out-of-the-body experiences. If the

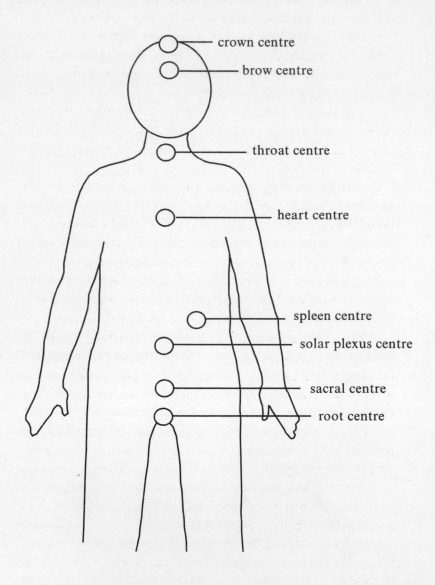

The psychic centres

centre is too open it can cause a feeling of being 'not quite there' or not properly grounded in the physical body.

The solar plexus centre is located just below the rib cage. All our emotions and sensations are registered at this centre. We talk about having a 'gut reaction' or getting 'butterflies' in the stomach if we are nervous. As the solar plexus is linked with the digestive system, any problems here can cause gastric upsets. Negative emotions such as fear and anger can become locked into this centre, causing tension and blockages that restrict the flow of energy.

Mediums are particularly vulnerable to disturbances at the solar plexus. Being sensitive, they react more strongly than most people to emotional hurts or attacks. If the centre is too open the medium will be picking up impressions all the time, from those around and from the astral level, with a consequent drain on the medium's vitality; hence the importance of 'closing down' after any psychic work (an exercise on how to 'close down' is given at the end of this chapter).

The heart centre is, as you would expect, linked to the physical heart. We speak of a person being 'open-hearted' or, if they are unkind, 'closing their heart' to someone in need. This is the centre of compassion and understanding. Provided you are working in sincerity and with a desire to be of service, it will unfold naturally. However, though sympathy for others is obviously needed, you need to guard against becoming too open, since this will make you over-sensitive to the emotions of those around you. Healers in particular have this difficulty and may pick up the physical conditions of their patients.

As the heart centre becomes activated it can release a lot of emotion. This is why those developing mediumship often find in the early stages that they are subject to erratic mood swings and fits of depression. This is also why you need to be emotionally stable before attempting to develop psychic gifts.

The throat and brow centres are the most important from the point of view of mediumship. The throat is used in clairaudience. It is also active in artists, writers and anyone with creative talents. The brow centre, which is also known as the third eye, governs clairvoyance. It is linked with the pineal and pituitary glands, those small, mysterious glands which are such a puzzle to scientists.

The crown centre is situated just above the head. In Eastern philosophy it is called the thousand-petalled lotus. The halo depicted in paintings above the heads of saints is a representation of this centre, which is bright and shining in a spiritually evolved person. Through this centre we are linked with our higher selves and the higher dimensions of the spirit world. If you keep your spiritual aspirations high this centre will open more and, as it does so, you will be drawn ever upwards towards the God force.

Linking all the centres together is a central column through which energy flows from the base of the spine to the crown of the head. This energy is called the *kundalini*. It is sometimes depicted as a serpent which lies coiled at the root chakra. As the chakras are stimulated by meditation or psychic development the serpent uncoils and rises up the spine, activating each of the centres in turn until it reaches the thousand-petalled lotus, where it is said to confer bliss and enlightenment.

Some in the New Age movement suggest that the *kundalini* is an extremely dangerous energy best left alone. This is not without foundation. If the *kundalini* is forced too rapidly up the spine, using certain yogic breathing exercises, it is like overloading an electrical circuit, and can cause physical and mental repercussions. However, the *kundalini* is to some extent active in every person. It is part of the system by which *prana* is distributed around the body and without it you wouldn't be alive. It is especially active in creative people, psychics and mediums, and in fact forms the basis of all psychic manifestations. If the mediumship is developed in the correct way, it will rise naturally during the course of development, enhancing the medium's power.

Exercise For Uncoiling The Serpent

The following exercise is a very good one to use at the beginning of a circle meeting as it will assist you to 'open' psychically and will make your mind receptive. It can be carried out by all the circle in unison, directed by the leader.

▷ Close your eyes, take a few deep breaths and, as you do so, relax the whole body. Start with your toes. Tense the muscles, then relax them. Bring your attention to your ankles and do the same. Work your way progressively up the body, tensing and relaxing each part in turn. Pay particular attention to the solar plexus and release any emotion you may be holding there. Finish with the eyes and the muscles of the face.

Now sit up straight, being careful not to tense up again, and make sure your spine is erect. Fix your attention on the base of your spine. Take a deep breath and, as you breathe in, imagine energy coming up from the earth, through the soles of your feet, up your legs and up to the base chakra. Picture the chakra like a flower opening and see if you can feel a gentle heat in this region.

Let the breath out and, as you breathe in again, draw the power up to the solar plexus centre and feel the petals opening. On the next breath take the energy up to the heart centre and so on through the throat and brow chakras, visualising each one in turn opening up. On the final breath take the power all the way up to the crown of the head, to the thousand-petalled lotus, then let it cascade like a fountain of light down through all the centres and through your entire body, filling it with vitality.

Rest for a short while, then bring your attention back to the crown centre. You have drawn up the earth energy. Now you are going to draw down the spiritual energy of the higher realms. Picture a golden light above your head and let that light descend to each of the chakras in turn. Feel it flooding every pore of your being with love. This light will give you increased energy and well-being. It is also your best protection against negativity, either physical or psychic. It forms a shield and any negativity that is directed towards you will bounce off it.

Feel the two streams of energy merging at the heart centre. The heart is the point of balance. If you picture the body as a cross, it would be the point where the two bars meet. When this centre is fully activated, everything you do will be motivated by love.

So, to finish, hold your attention steady at the heart. Send out your thoughts to those in the spirit world, asking that they will blend their energies with yours and assist you to meet on the rainbow bridge.

Guides And Mediums

When you start sitting in a development circle you will no doubt be told that you have various guides with you. Monks and nuns are particular favourites and, of course, there are the inevitable Native Americans and Chinamen.

These descriptions give rise to derisive laughter in sceptics, but as a medium myself I do see such figures. In fact, I am aware of a nun who works very closely with me. So I do believe that there are beings on the astral plane who undertake the task – and a very thankless one it must be – of working with mediums in this way. As to the exotic costumes – they may have been Native Americans, Chinamen or whatever when they were on earth. We are told that many guides are drawn from races that, when on earth, had much spiritual wisdom and a natural aptitude for communication with the spirit world.

But I am sure that they themselves have no need of these earthly trappings. The dress in which we see them is a form adopted for our benefit rather than theirs. They come from a dimension where the concept of personality no longer applies but, like an actor donning a costume in which he will be recognised, they show themselves to us in a way that we can accept. A guide may just as easily have been an English person, but mediums are taught to expect Native Americans and the like, so that is the form they obligingly adopt.

Guides often say that they are members of a soul group, a closely knit family of souls who, after many lifetimes as individuals, are beginning to merge as one entity. These groups are working on various spiritual planes to help humanity. The guide is their link with the earth, through whom their collective wisdom can be transmitted. The medium may be a member of the same group, in which case the affinity between them will be very strong and consequently it will be easier for them to communicate.

Every medium has a group of guides around them who help the medium in their work. This group may change from time to time. Some only stay with the medium for a short while or come to fulfil a particular purpose. Others remain throughout the medium's life. These are the main guides and the relationship with them is a very special one. They become loved and trusted friends, and though they do not live the medium's life for them or make decisions in mundane affairs, they are always there in the background, quietly supporting and directing.

The guides are in charge of a medium's development. They attune the mind and stimulate the psychic centres. When the medium is working, they provide a link with the spirit communicators, who can be just as confused, emotional and ignorant of the mechanism of communication as those on earth and would be unable to make contact directly.

Guides also do a lot of work behind the scenes. For instance, when a person arranges a sitting with a medium they will try to ensure that, as far as possible, those in the spirit world most closely connected with them, or those they most want to hear from, will be present. They prepare the medium mentally and, if necessary, prepare the atmosphere of the place where the medium is going to work. So, though a sitting may seem to be a haphazard affair, with the medium 'bringing through' whoever happens to be there at the time, it is in fact all carefully orchestrated. And I imagine that, as on earth, the quiet workers in the background have the hardest job and receive the least recognition.

Exercise For Getting To Know Your Guide

The most important contact you have to make as a medium is with your guide. Once you know the being who is working with you, you can form a partnership that will lead you through all your difficulties, facilitate your contact with other communicators, and steer your life and work for as long as you remain on earth. This exercise will help you to get to know your guide.

▷ Sit quietly, either in the circle or in your own private meditation time and ask to be made aware of the guide who is in change of your development, then wait and see what comes into your mind. Do not have any prior expectations of what they will be like and don't be disappointed if you don't see a 6 foot Native American! You may get a name or see a mental picture, or you may receive just an impression of a personality.

However it comes, hold that link steady in your mind. Concentrate your thoughts like a beam of light going out over the rainbow bridge towards the guide. Allow your mind to merge with your guide's. Feel yourself being carried over that bridge until you meet on the other side and be attentive to whatever thoughts or ideas come into your head.

If you are in the circle, then, with the permission of your circle leader, you may care to speak these words or thoughts aloud. This is called 'inspired speaking' and may deepen into trance (both these aspects are explained in Chapter 11). Every time you begin your meditation and each time before you give a sitting or take a meeting call upon your guide or guides to help you. They are your strength, and if you work in love and sincerity they will never let you down.

When you first join a circle you may feel a little awkward or embarrassed, not knowing what to expect or what is expected of you. This is especially so if you are invited as a new member to a well-established group. At least you should know enough about mediumship by now to realise that you are not going to see spirits popping up all over the place!

In fact, for the first few weeks you may not see or sense anything at all. Don't worry about this. Allow yourself time to settle into the routine of the group. Do the exercise to open the psychic centres given earlier in this chapter, then just sit quietly, absorbing the peace and allowing your mind to become still. Even if you have been in the habit of meditating regularly at home, it takes a while to get used to meditating within a group and to discipline your mind to ignore all the little distractions – coughs and creaking of chairs – that are bound to occur when a group of people are sitting together.

If the circle is a newly formed one for beginners, the leader may well spend the first few weeks or even months in practising the sort of exercises in psychic awareness outlined in Chapter 8. This is a necessary first step. Before you can begin to develop mediumship, you have to get the psychic powers functioning. In some people these are so deeply buried that it takes a long time to bring them to the surface.

When mediumship does begin to manifest it seldom comes in a dramatic way. Nearly always it starts with sensing. In my own case – and most of the mediums I have spoken to had the same sort of experience – I would get a vague sense of a communicator with me, just enough to say whether it was a man or a woman, and to get a general indication of their personality. If I was lucky, I might hear a few words in my mind. I was very hesitant to share these impressions with the rest of the group in case I was wrong, but when I did find the courage to speak out I was surprised how often the spirit people I described could be recognised and accepted by someone present. This gave me confidence and, as my confidence improved, so the 'messages' came through more strongly.

But how are these impressions actually received? It's

worth considering this because, the more you understand what is going on, the better you can co-operate with your spirit helpers.

When you sense a communicator close to you, it is because they have come within your aura and have harmonised their vibrations with yours, in a sense overshadowing you. This enables you to glean certain basic information about them. For instance, if the communicator is a big person you will feel yourself getting bigger. If they had a military bearing you will have an urge to sit up straight and put your shoulders back. You may also get a sense of what they died of. Someone who had a chest complaint might give you a momentary sensation of fighting for breath, but this should only be momentary, as it is just a memory for them, not something they are still suffering from.

The reason why mediumship starts in this way has to do with the psychic centres. The process of development stimulates the *kundalini* power to rise up from the base of the spine. As it reaches the solar plexus centre, that centre becomes activated. This is where sensations are registered, so in this early stage you will 'sense', picking up a general idea of what sort of person is communicating and feeling something of their personality and emotions.

Exercise To Improve Clairsentience

▷ As you feel the communicator there, send out a positive thought to them rather than passively waiting for them to do all the work. Speak to them in your mind, acknowledging what you are receiving. Be very attentive to the sensations you are getting. Try to 'hone in' on these, like fine-tuning a radio, so as to make them more precise. Speak to the communicator

in your mind and ask them questions about themselves. It doesn't matter if you don't get an answer.
By speaking in this way you are helping to strengthen
your mental link with them. Listen for any words
you may hear and watch for any picture that may
flash across the screen of your mind. Although this
level of mediumship is concerned with emotion and
sensation, none of the centres work in isolation, and
words and pictures may also come to you.

Tell the other members of the group what you are
getting, however silly or unlikely it may sound to
you. This is the only way to test whether you are
getting it right. It also helps your spirit friends to
know how much of the information they are trying
to put across is actually getting through to you.

As the *kundalini* energy rises, it touches the other psychic
centres in ascending order. This usually happens unconsciously although, if you constantly practise the exercise
for uncoiling the serpent, you may be aware of a gentle heat
rising up your spine. When the power reaches the higher
psychic centres, the throat and the brow, the mediumship
begins to function at the levels of clairaudience (the throat)
and clairvoyance (the 'third eye' centre between the eyebrows) and these begin to unfold. It then becomes possible to use these abilities in a regular, controlled way, rather
than relying on the rare 'flashes' of vision or occasional
voices which are a feature of natural, undeveloped mediumship.

Few mediums have the faculties of clairvoyance and
clairaudience developed to an equal degree. Nearly always
one or the other will predominate. Which one it is depends on
the type of mind you have. If you are a visual person, clairvoyance will come most naturally. If, like me, your mind
works in words rather than pictures, you will be mainly

clairaudient. Both gifts can be improved by practice. Obviously, the one which does not come easily to you will need the most work.

Exercise To Improve Clairaudience

A good way of practicing this exercise is for the members of the group to sit in pairs and take it in turns to attempt to pass on communications to each other.

▷ Sit opposite your partner but do not concentrate on them. Take a moment to be still and fix your attention on the throat centre. Ask your guides to bring a communicator to you whom your partner will be able to recognise. Listen intently for any words or names that come to you. Do not expect these to be external; they will be heard within your head. Repeat to your partner exactly what you hear or what you think you are hearing. If it doesn't make much sense to you, don't try to interpret it in any way; this is how so much communication gets distorted. What seems like nonsense to you may be very meaningful to the recipient. If you don't quite catch the words – sometimes they come very fast – ask for them to be repeated.

This exercise requires a lot of concentration and can be frustrating when nothing comes but it is well worth persevering with. If you establish a clear link in this way, the information received has a sharpness and clarity that distinguishes it from the thoughts that arise from the subconscious mind.

Exercise To Improve Clairvoyance

Clairvoyance can be practised in the same way. Again, sit opposite your partner. This time fix your attention on the brow centre. You may see objectively, that is to say, with your eyes open, though, of course, it is really your inner eyes that are being used.

▷ Again, ask your guides to bring a communicator your partner will recognise. Do not look directly at your partner but try to sense who is standing behind or beside them. Don't expect an apparition to appear! You are more likely to perceive a hazy out-line or to get an impression that is half-way between seeing and sensing. Describe what you see in as much detail as you can.

Now close your eyes and imagine you had a tele-vision screen inside your head, at the point between the eyebrows. Can you see any pictures on the screen? You might see faces, scenes or objects, or even a colour. These mental pictures tend to come and go very fast. If necessary, ask to be shown them again. As with the exercise for clairaudience, at first there will be a lot of interference from your subcon-scious, but in time this will sort itself out as the im-pressions from spirit come through more clearly.

Closing Down

Earlier in this chapter I gave an exercise for opening up the psychic centres. It is equally important to 'close down'. This should be done at the end of every circle meeting and every time you have been working psychically. While you are open, you are using your psychic energy. If you do not 'close down' your physical as well as your psychic vitality will become drained. There are various ways of 'closing down'. I always find the following exercise simple and effective.

▷ Concentrate on each of the chakras in turn, beginning at the top of your head, and visualise each one as a flower. See the petals of the flower closing. Pay particular attention to the solar plexus centre as this is the most vulnerable. When you have mentally closed all the chakras, start once more at the head. Visualise a golden light above your head and draw it all the way down to your feet, enclosing you like a cloak.

Thank your guides for working with you and send out a prayer for all those in need, and for the whole planet. Finally, bring yourself completely back to earth by having something to eat or drink.

In the next chapter we will look at further aspects of mediumship and see how some of the common difficulties that arise can be dealt with.

10

WORKING AS A
MEDIUM

Sceptics frequently allege that mediums get all their information by tapping into the mind of the sitter. This allegation does not stand up when you consider that mediums are able to give facts of which the sitter is unaware or to describe spirit communicators whom they do not know but whose existence they are subsequently able to verify. However, the sceptics do have a valid point.

Linking With Spirit

I have described mediumship as a form of telepathy between the minds of those on earth and those in spirit. Mediums are trained to be receptive to the thoughts that are transmitted to them. But the sitter's mind is also broadcasting thoughts and the medium may inadvertently pick these up as well. This problem cannot be entirely eliminated but, by using your mediumistic faculty in the right way, it is possible to guard against it and ensure that what you give a sitter really does come from the spirit.

To do this, there is one golden rule. Make your link

with spirit and not with the sitter. Let me explain what I mean.

As a medium you cannot help but be very sensitive to other people. When you sit down with a sitter and open your psychic centres you will feel impressions flowing from them. You will not be able to read their minds exactly, which is perhaps just as well, but you will be able to sense quite a lot about their personality and also detect such things as what sort of mood they are in or whether they have any aches and pains. This is called 'auric reading'. You don't have to actually see the person's aura but you are in fact blending your aura with theirs, so you cannot help but be sensitive to their thoughts and feelings.

Some mediums do auric reading without being aware of it. This lack of understanding accounts for the low standard of mediumship that is so prevalent today. Eileen Roberts, the president of the Institute of Spiritualist Mediums, says: 'A lot of people who are psychic think they are in touch with spirit when they're not. All they are doing is to tap into the sitters' auras, like dipping into a bran tub and picking up thoughts and images at random.'

Why should this be so important? First, because it's not true communication. Eileen says, 'If you don't make contact with spirit then you are not a channel for the divine power. You are just touching the frayed edges of it.'

Second, it can be dangerously misleading since it is possible, even with the best of intentions, to pick a strong desire in the sitter's mind and relay it back as a 'spirit message'.

Suppose, for example, that a sitter comes to you who wants guidance with a problem in a relationship. You tell her that everything is going to turn out well because you honestly believe that is what you are getting from your guides. She goes away happy, but a couple of weeks later she comes back, highly indignant, to tell you that her partner has ran off with another woman and demanding to know

why you got it wrong. What happened is that you unconsciously tuned into her instead of spirit and were influenced
by her strong feelings about what she wanted to happen.
Had you been properly attuned to spirit, you would not have
made such a mistake.

The following exercise is a useful one to practise in the
circle by the members sitting in pairs and taking it in turns
to act as medium and sitter. It will help you to tell the difference between the different levels of perception. It is in two
parts.

▷   Sit opposite your partner. It is better if the partner
    can be someone you do not know well. Focus your
    attention at your solar plexus centre. Feel your
    aura expand so that it embraces the aura of the
    other person. It may help to link hands with them.
    What do you sense emanating from them? This is
    rather like the exercise in psychometry given in
    Chapter 8, except that you are using a person in-
    stead of an object. What sort of personality are
    they? Are they happy or sad, depressed or elated?
    What sort of family do they have? What do they
    do for the living? Don't think about spirit com-
    munication at this point or try to think with your
    guide. Just concentrate on what you feel emanating
    from the person.

    Have a short break to clear your mind, then go on
    to the next part of the exercise.

    This time, don't look at your partner. Ignore them
    as far as possible. Focus your attention on your
    throat and brow centres, and ask your guide to bring
    a communicator to you whom your partner will rec-
    ognise. Don't say anything until you feel that there is
    someone there, then pass on whatever comes to you,
    however you receive it. Concentrate only on the

communicator and on the information they are transmitting to you.

Notice that these two methods of working have a very different 'feel' about them. It is much easier to tune into a sitter. Tuning into spirit requires more mental effort because it is a higher level of vibration. But to be able to do this, clearly and consistently, is the mark of a good and conscientious medium.

Common Problems Encountered By Budding Mediums

Though each person is unique in the way in which their gifts unfold, there are certain problems and difficulties that are experienced by nearly all budding mediums. So I thought it might be helpful if I listed some of these and suggested solutions.

The first problem is encountered by healers as well as mediums, in fact, by anyone who develops their psychic ability.

How can I prevent myself from becoming too sensitive?

The process of development affects you on all levels, physical and emotional as well as psychic. You will find that you get tired more easily than before. You also become more deeply affected by the moods and sufferings of others. If you have a healing gift you will be inclined to 'pick up' the health conditions of those around you. Crowded places become hard to tolerate; loud noises jar on your ears. You can find yourself getting tense and irritable.

Well, you said you wanted to be a medium and this is

the price you pay for it! If you were not sensitive to a high degree, you couldn't be aware of the spirit world. However, it is possible to guard against the worst effects. The first and most practical solution is to allow yourself plenty of rest, and make sure you eat a good, wholesome diet. Many people consider that a vegetarian diet has a refining effect on psychic ability, but this is a matter of individual preference and you must decide what is best for you.

Consider also taking a good vitamin and mineral supplement. Vitamin B complex is particularly good for restoring your vitality when you are depleted on a psychic level. Bach flower remedies are also very helpful. These may be purchased from most health food shops. They are prepared from the distilled essence of flowers and plants, and are designed to act on the underlying mental states that cause stress, disharmony and disease. There is also a fairly new range of flower and crystal essences which, like the Bach flower remedies, are designed to restore balance and harmony to the mind and spirit as well as the body. These are not so readily available but are sold in shops selling psychic books and artefacts, and are available at psychic fairs. (The addresses of a supplier is given in the Useful Addresses list at the back of this book.) These essences can help to open and balance the chakras.

Keep yourself calm and free from stress as far as you can. Regular meditation will help with this. But, above all, close down psychically using the exercise at the end of Chapter 9. In the early stages, you need to do this exercise several times a day, every time after working psychically, at the end of every circle meeting, and whenever you finish meditating. It is easy to open without realising you have done so; just talking about psychic matters will cause this to happen. Go through the exercise in your mind whenever you feel your vitality becoming drained.

How do I know if I've closed down properly?

It's easier to explain how you can tell if you haven't! If you are constantly 'picking up' impressions or seeing and hearing spirit, then you are allowing yourself to be too open. When you close, you can feel your aura contracting. There is a sense of coming down to earth, of being fully anchored in the psychical world. You may think that your guides should do the closing down for you – after all, they are there to protect you. They will do what they can, but in the main this is your responsibility. Some people say, 'I can't stop the spirit world from intruding.' But you can stop it, if you want to. Just tell them to go away! You are not a mere passive instrument. You must be in control of your mediumship at all times.

I don't seem to be making any progress in the development circle – am I doing something wrong?

Probably not. Every medium I have spoken to has said that development goes by fits and starts. You seem to be getting on well, then you reach a stage where your progress halts. If anything you feel as if you are going backwards. If you have reached one of these stages, don't despair. See it as a plateau where you can assimilate what you have learned so far. Sooner or later, if you are patient, you will take another leap forward.

Should you feel, after a few months of sitting in the circle, that you are not really getting anywhere, it may be that you are just not cut out to be a medium. This doesn't indicate any inadequacy on your part. You may have some other latent gift, such as healing or public speaking. These gifts are just as valuable a way of using your link with the spirit world. If you are motivated by a desire to serve, your spirit helpers will guide you to do whatever you are most suited for.

How can I tell the difference between spirit communication and my own imagination?

This question comes up more than any other. It is a problem all mediums have, especially in the early stages. The only way to learn the difference is by trial and error. 'Give off' whatever you receive, and see what is accepted and what is not. In time you will notice that what is given by spirit has greater clarity than the words and images that float up from your subconscious. Avoid working at times when you are tired or under stress as this dulls your perception. Also, avoid straining for any particular piece of information or to get the answer to a specific question. If this is not forthcoming from spirit, your imagination will rush to fill the gap and this causes a lot of confusion.

How can I get clearer communication?

The basic answer to this is by practice and hard work, which will attune your mind more and more finely. However, there is one exercise that was suggested to me by Eileen Roberts at one of her seminars and I have found it very helpful. It is set out below.

Exercise To Get Clearer Communication

▷   When you feel a communicator trying to make contact with you, invite them to come within your aura, as it were, to stand in your shoes, so that you occupy the same mental space. Concentrate on them until you feel that you almost become that person. Close your eyes if it helps your concentration – never mind the sitter! Let the emotions, words and images flow through you as if they were your own.

This may seem a simple exercise but it is a very powerful one. Many mediums have told me that they are now working in this way. It seems that the spirit world is initiating this change to a deeper level of contact. It is very clear and definite, and makes all the difference between *wondering* whether what you are getting is correct and *knowing* that it is because the attunement is so close.

Should I pass on everything I receive, even if it's bad news?

It is always difficult to know whether or not to pass on some message which you know is not what the sitter wants to hear. Sometimes a communicator may wish to give a warning of a future event and in this case you must use your discretion as to how you convey the warning. Try not to say anything that will distress the sitter. For instance, I would never predict a death, even if I was given this sort of information, which I very rarely am. If you work in love, you will be guided as to what to say and what to leave out. Think how you would feel if you were on the receiving end!

Working In Public

How do I know when I'm ready to start working in public?

Your circle leader will help you or you will receive a strong prompting from your guides. Going from a small, private development circle to a public platform in a church or at a spiritualist meeting is a daunting experience. Some churches offer evenings which are called 'open platforms' or 'fledgling nights'. This is a half-way stage, where those who have been sitting in a circle for a period of time can practise their mediumship in front of a sympathetic audience. Though still nerve-racking, it is better than being thrown in at the deep end. One medium told me how she started: 'The person who was supposed to be taking the service didn't turn up and I was "volunteered". I was so nervous my knees were knocking! But once I stood up it just flowed and since then I haven't looked back.'

I have heard similar stories from so many mediums that I think it must be the spirit world's favourite way of getting people launched, especially those timid souls who would never push themselves forward. So be warned – it could happen to you!

Starting out

If you are just beginning your public work, it's best to start in a small way. However much you may be inspired with zeal to spread the word, don't book the Albert Hall! If you belong to a spiritualist church, start there or find a small, friendly church where you can offer your services, perhaps initially sharing your platform with a more experienced medium who can help you out if you get into difficulties or run out of steam.

Working on a public platform presents the greatest challenge a medium can face. It is easier in a spiritualist church, where you are in the main preaching to the converted and where you can draw upon the psychic energy that has been built up. Public meetings held in theatres or halls are far more difficult. Mediums such as Doris Collins, Stephen O'Brien and the late Doris Stokes have done much to bring the knowledge of life after death to those who would never dream of entering a church, spiritualist or otherwise, but not many mediums have their confidence or stamina.

You may prefer to begin your work by giving private sittings in your own home. This is less stressful in that you do not have to stand up and speak in front of strangers, but it brings its own problems. There is the very practical consideration, especially if you are a woman on your own, that you have to be very careful where you advertise and whom you invite into your home.

Before you begin you need to prepare both yourself and the room where you are going to work. If you can put aside a room of your home just for sittings, this is ideal. If you do not have enough space for this, choose a room which is normally quiet and peaceful. Keep it clean and tidy and uncluttered. A couple of comfortable chairs and perhaps a table are all you need. Fresh flowers and spiritual pictures help to create the right atmosphere. When you have it looking as you wish, dedicate it to the service of God and the world of spirit, asking that whoever comes into it will receive according to their needs. Ask your guides also to put a ring of protection around the room. However carefully you vet your sitters, you can't tell what sort of spirit people they are going to bring with them! As long as you are working in light and love, no undesirable forces will be allowed to intrude.

Meditate and pray in your room daily. Over a period of time you will feel the atmosphere becoming charged with psychic energy. This energy will touch all your sitters, even if they are not aware of it, so that they will go out feeling strengthened by the presence of spirit, as well as by any help you may have been able to give them during the sitting.

Make a little time, before each sitter arrives, to sit quietly in the room, attune to spirit and the psychic centres. The spirit friends and relatives of the sitter sometimes arrive before they do, so you may be able to make a mental link with them then. Try to put all distractions out of your mind, and make yourself calm and receptive.

Some sitters can be very demanding and come armed with a string of questions or a desperate desire to contact some particular person whom you may be unable to contact. Do not allow yourself to be put under pressure. Every sitting should be regarded as an experiment. It is your responsibility to work in honesty and to do your best for everyone who comes to you, but the sitter also has a responsibility to approach the sitting with a sympathetic, open-minded attitude, and to accept that you can only relay to them what you are able to receive.

Even experienced mediums have some blank sittings. The only honest thing to do when this happens is to admit that you are getting nothing and ask the sitter to return at some other time or recommend them to another medium. It may be that you are just having an 'off' day because of tiredness or ill health, or perhaps you are allowing your nerves to get in the way. But don't assume that it is necessarily your fault. The sitter may be setting up a mental barrier because of a sceptical or negative attitude. Excessive emotion on their part can also create a barrier. Someone who is depleted can drain your vitality so that you have no psychic energy to work with. Don't be too discouraged. You can't win them all!

Clearing the room

After your sitter has gone, you should cleanse the room psychically to clear any negativity from the atmosphere. This is rather like opening the window to get rid of the smell of cigarettes or perfume visitors may leave behind.

▷ Stand in the centre of the room and send out a prayer for the sitter and for those in spirit who have come with them. Close down psychically. Then visualise a white light descending from your crown centre and spreading out to fill the entire room.

The Rewards Of Mediumship

One of the things you will very quickly discover about doing this work is that it teaches you more about people in this world than those in the next. I have met some delightful people and made some wonderful friends, but I have also come across my share of oddities and sitters who don't have the faintest idea of what a medium is supposed to do. One young woman brushed aside attempts to talk about her grandparents whom I could sense with her.

'I don't care about them, they're dead. I want to know what's going to happen to me!'

It's futile to point out to people like this that a medium is not a fortune-teller. They've come to have their fortunes told and anything to do with the spirit world is quite irrelevant!

Another woman arrived with a pools coupon in her hand. 'I need some money to settle my debts,' she informed me, 'so if you could just tell me which numbers to fill in . . .'

She was disappointed when I replied, 'If I could do that I wouldn't be sitting here talking to you. I'd be on a yacht in the Bahamas!'

But perhaps that's not as bad as the experience of a friend of mine whose sitter was desperate to contact her late husband. Imagining, mistakenly, that it would help the medium if she brought along an article belonging to him, she had brought his false teeth!

I have spoken a lot about the difficulties of mediumship but what are the rewards? These are great, and far outweigh the problems and frustrations. I wouldn't change the work I do. It has brought me some tears, but it has also brought me love and laughter, and there is no other way of life I would find so satisfying or worthwhile.

Stephen O'Brien, Britain's most celebrated medium, has said, 'Soul satisfaction is the medium's reward – to feel that you have helped someone to find a little comfort, a little light in the darkness of their depression of grief. It is a tremendous sense of joy that one has been able to kindle within the souls who have come to witness the mediumship new hope for tomorrow and new strength to carry on with the great adventure of life.'

There is one vital point I want to make and that is that you cannot separate yourself from your mediumship. The sort of person you are determines the kind of mediumship you will produce. A person who is shallow and insincere will only produce superficial 'messages'. If you go within and cultivate your spiritual as well as your psychic qualities, what you are able to give will be at a deeper level.

These days, increasing demands are being made on mediums. The evidence of survival after death is still needed and always will be, to comfort the newly bereaved and convince those who are seeking for evidence, but this is no longer enough. With the general increase in psychic awareness among people, mediums must have sufficient knowledge to be able to guide those who are perplexed or having experiences they find frightening, and to show them how to use their psychic abilities in the best way.

The time may come when everyone can make their own contacts in the spirit world and mediums are redundant, but I will be quite happy about that. To me, this is the purpose of mediumship; to teach people how to communicate with the spirit world for themselves, and also how to find their own spirit within, in order to live lives that are happier and more fulfilled.

For the final chapter of this book I want to look at an aspect of mediumship I have not so far mentioned. Trance is an unusual phenomenon and requires great dedication, but it is perhaps the highest form of mediumship.

11

TRANCE

Many people think that going into a trance is what mediums do as a matter of course. This may have been the case 50 or 100 years ago, but it is no longer true today. Trance mediums are a rarity and those that do work in this way are often reluctant to demonstrate their gifts on a public platform.

Trance looks very easy. Theoretically, all you have to do is sit there and go to sleep, while your guide 'comes through' and does all the work for you. If it was really as simple as that I'd do it all the time! In fact, it usually requires a lot of training and self-discipline to link with the spirit world in this way. And not every medium has the ability to do it. But whether or not you have aspirations in this direction, it's worth studying the phenomenon because it does throw a very interesting light on the mechanics of communication.

The trouble with trance is that unless it is done well it can look and sound ridiculous. I remember a demonstration I witnessed at a spiritualist meeting, many years ago. The medium, a plump, Madame Arcati type woman, was something of a celebrity. Certainly, she had a devoted following. She sat in the centre of a darkened stage, her eyes tightly closed, her hands gripping the arms of the chair. The audience, tense and expectant, sat in respectful silence. There was a long wait, then she began to writhe as if in pain. A series of groans issued from her lips. I thought she was about to have a fit, but no one else seemed particularly alarmed. This, the man beside me confided in a whisper, was what always happened when her guide, Big Chief Sitting Bull or whatever his name was, came through. A few moments later, she rose to her feet, her eyes still closed. Majestically, she raised her hand and a voice, deafening in its intensity, burst from her lips; 'How!'

The discourse that followed owed very little to inspiration and a great deal to imagination. As her talk was peppered with expressions like 'white man speak with forked tongue' I can only assume she had been watching too many westerns. I don't know what sort of impression she made on the rest of the audience. I was torn between a desire to walk out in disgust and an almost irrepressible urge to laugh.

But I have seen other mediums, such as Ivy Northage and Ursula Roberts, who are in a completely different category and are held in great respect. They do not indulge in any of these ridiculous theatricals and when their spirit teachers speak through them the listeners have a real and moving sense of being in direct contact with a higher dimension of life.

What Makes A Trance Medium?

Why do some people develop this faculty while others are completely unable to do so, no matter how hard they try? This seems to depend on one's psychic constitution. In order for the guide to take control, the medium's etheric body has to withdraw slightly from the physical. Some mediums have what is termed a 'loose' etheric body that can move out of the physical very easily. The medium is then effectively asleep and has no knowledge of what is being said through him or her. To reach this state of trance can take years of patient training. It is, as I have said, rare and most mediums never work in this way, although they often go into a light trance in which they are still aware of what is going on. When deep trance occurs suddenly it can be very frightening, as Mary Absolum discovered.

Mary, who now works at the College of Psychic Studies in London, was in her twenties when, due to a combination of distressing circumstances, she attempted to commit suicide. Some five years later, by which time she had managed to rebuild her life, she was invited to join a development circle. She accepted with some reluctance as she had no particular interest in spiritualism, but she quite enjoyed sitting with the group so she continued to attend. One evening she thought she had fallen asleep and was amazed when she was told that she had been in trance.

I was terrified! I was convinced that I was possessed. I used to sit up all night with the lights on, afraid to go to sleep. No one in the circle did anything to reassure me. 'Don't worry about it, dear,' they told me, but I *was* worried. Something was happening to me that I couldn't control. I was afraid it would happen at inconvenient times, like at work or when I was on the bus.

Fortunately, this never happened, but for a long time she kept her fears to herself until a friend in whom she confided and who was knowledgeable on the subject undertook to give her a proper training. This was long and demanding; it was at least two years before she felt competent to give trance sittings.

Mary believes that it is significant that her ability began

to surface some time after her suicide attempt. 'I think the crisis released my contact with my subconscious powers. It started the change in my brain patterns that made my close contact with the spirit world possible.'

Some trance mediums can trace their gift back to childhood. Clive Daniels, a well-known medium who has been working in this field for many years, said, 'When I was a young boy I would often collapse with fainting fits. While I was unconscious I would be jabbering away in an unknown tongue. My step-mother was naturally worried but when she called in the doctor, all he said was "He'll grow out of it!"'

Clive was a sensitive child, and often saw and described spirit people, much to the consternation of his step-mother who told him not to be silly. He also regularly saw an oriental man whom he later came to recognise as his guide, Woo Wang. Some years later he learned that his natural mother, who had died young, had been a medium. When he was 15 he joined a development circle.

> I was aware of Woo Wang standing beside me. As he
> was speaking I could hear the words coming out of
> my mouth. I was petrified and vowed that I was never
> going to let that happen again and it never did. After
> that he always took me over completely, which I
> found much more comfortable.

It might be asked why guides, who are presumably such loving beings, subject their mediums to these unpleasant experiences. The answer may be that it is the only way in which they can make the initial contact and that the fear is caused only by the medium's lack of knowledge or understanding. Clive feels that, in his own case, it was a way of overcoming his shyness and that, if he hadn't been taken over in this way, he would never have had the courage to work in public.

What does it feel like to go into a trance? Basically, it's like falling asleep. Time and time again mediums say that the first time it happened to them was when they were sitting in circle; they thought they had fallen asleep and were somewhat embarrassed – then they were told that someone had been speaking through them. Some mediums see a light as they drift off. Few recall any dreams or out-of-the-body experiences in this state, although this can sometimes happen. Clive feels that, while Woo Wang is in charge, he is standing nearby in his spirit body.

It has been questioned whether the guides who work with trance mediums, or any mediums for that matter, exist as separate entities in their own right or whether they are thought creations, split-off portions of the medium's own personality. This is something parapsychologists may argue over. To mediums themselves there is no doubt. Their guides are definite individuals with whom they have a close bond of love and trust. In fact, if there were not a basic soul affinity between them the partnership could not work.

The connection may go back to a past life. Medium and guide may be members of the same soul group, and have shared many earthly lifetimes together, but whether or not this is the case, the medium will have been carefully selected as the most suitable channel for the particular guide who wants to work with them. Mary once asked her guide, a Chinese mandarin, why he chose her and was told, not very flatteringly, 'You were a cracked vessel but you were the best I could find!'

To watch a trance medium working is to witness a dramatic transformation. The medium in effect becomes a different person. Their voice and intonation change, and they employ gestures and mannerisms quite unlike their usual behaviour. A clairvoyant observing the medium should be able to see or sense the guide that is present.

Colouring

It is not too difficult to distinguish between true trance and the self-induced variety where the medium, like the one I described at the beginning of this chapter, has been carried away by their own imagination. With the latter, it takes only a slight degree of psychic awareness to discern that there is 'nothing there' and that the 'communications' are emanating solely from the medium's subconscious. Vacuous speeches, full of platitudes, are warning signs, as are Native Americans who say 'How!'. There is, however, a grey area where the medium has a partial contact with a guide, but the message is being coloured or distorted by the medium's mind.

In fact, however good or sincere the medium, there is always some degree of colouring or distortion. This is unavoidable because of the way trance works. It is a process that requires great skill and delicacy on the part of the spirit operators. The guide has first to cause the medium's etheric body to withdraw partially or completely. The guide's mind then has to blend with the medium's so that the medium will speak the words as the guide transmits. Because they are unconscious, it might be thought that the medium's mind would play no part in what is being said, but this is not quite true. The subconscious is still the channel through which the transmission comes and can still influence it to some extent. The deeper the trance the less the interference but it can never be entirely eliminated.

The Changing Mechanics Of Trance

Looking back at the great mediums of the past, it becomes apparent that the mechanics of trance have changed over the years. In the nineteenth century this was the usual way of working and seems to have been of a deeper degree than is common today. The guides would completely take over the medium's physical body, manipulating the larynx and lungs, and controlling the medium's movements. This placed a great strain on the medium who often suffered from exhaustion afterwards. It was also extremely dangerous, since if the medium was touched or startled by a sudden noise while in this state the jolt would cause severe nervous shock. One of the famous early mediums, Mrs Gladys Osborne Leonard, was once almost asphyxiated when the spirit controlling her forgot to breathe!

It is hardly surprising that mediums became unwilling to put themselves through this ordeal and this probably explains why deep trance went out of fashion, being replaced by a more mental form of control. Even so, there is still an element of danger. Clive recalls an occasion when, just as he was finishing his demonstration, the chairperson touched his arm in order to help him back to his chair: 'It gave me such a terrible shock that I screamed. My arm was black and blue for two weeks afterwards.'

Now, whenever he works in public, he makes sure that he has someone responsible sitting beside him to ensure this does not happen. But many mediums are understandably not prepared to take the risk of being injured in this way and save their deep trance work for private gatherings.

Fears About Trance

Newcomers to circles are often confused by this form of mediumship. They feel they can't be proper mediums unless they can 'do' trance and are disappointed when it doesn't come. There may also be a fear lurking in the back of their minds that they will be possessed – taken over against their will, unable to control who comes through or what they say. Fortunately, this fear is quite unfounded. Trance is not the same as possession, in which a person is taken over by a malignant entity. Possession cannot happen to anyone who is sane and well balanced. If you are seeking in sincerity you will attract wise and loving helpers who will protect you.

Another fear people have is that they might drift off and never get back! This is really the least of your problems. The trance state is difficult to maintain for more than a few minutes in the early stages. Should it be necessary, your circle leader will gently call you back and, even if this was not done, you would fall into a natural sleep and wake up in the normal way.

However, unless you are that rare phenomenon, a natural trance medium, it is unlikely that you will plunge into a deep trance the moment you sit down in the circle. If it comes at all, it will come gradually as you bring your mind more in harmony with your guides.

Degrees Of Trance

There are, as I have indicated, varying degrees of trance. You can slip into a light trance whenever you are relaxed, daydreaming perhaps, or listening to music. In this state the conscious mind becomes still and the inner senses are less inhibited. At such times it is easier to become aware of the spirit world. Clairvoyant mediums are often in a light trance, though they may not even be aware of it.

Nearly everyone who sits in a circle is familiar with the light trance sensation. It is that pleasant, dreamy state when you are peacefully meditating. You are fully conscious but everything seems to have receded a little. A trance like this is easily broken. Someone coughs or your nose itches and instantly you are fully awake again. But as you begin to go into a slightly deeper state the sensations change slightly.

Now both mind and body are more deeply relaxed. Any sounds in the room seem to come from somewhere far away. It is rather like being hypnotised. You know you could move or open your eyes but it is too much effort. In a sense, you are being hypnotised, but by your guide. What is happening is that your guide is raising your level of consciousness in order to bring you into harmony with his or her vibrations.

This state is called 'control' or 'overshadowing'. I don't like the word 'control' since it is not very accurate. The guide is not manipulating you as if you were a puppet, but blending his or her mind with yours. The term 'overshadowing' is more appropriate because it does feel like a cloak being thrown over you mentally.

Sometimes it is enough just to let yourself rest in this state, enjoying the communication with spirit. At other times you may feel inspired to speak. 'Inspired speaking', as it is called, is as close to deep trance as most mediums get. That is not to suggest any shortcoming on their part. It may be as much as the spirit world requires of them.

Developing Inspired Speaking

You should not attempt to develop any form of trance or inspired speaking while sitting alone. Without an experienced person to look after you, you may be tempted to sit for far too long, since the sensation is such a peaceful one, and this will drain your vitality. There is also a slight danger of an unsuitable communicator trying to overshadow you. I do not mean evil entities, since your purity of intention and your sanity will safeguard you against this sort of intrusion. But there is a possibility that you might attract a less evolved entity who might be reluctant to go away again.

The best place to practise is in your circle, where the energy generated by the group will assist you. Before seeking to develop this gift, however, you should discuss your intention with your circle leader. When the group as a whole is meditating, it is very distracting if one member suddenly starts speaking, however beautiful or inspired the words. If the circle leader agrees, arrange a particular time, perhaps immediately after the meditation period, when you will try to let your guide come through. If several members of the circle all wish to practise this, you could arrange to take it in turns.

▷ Begin by sitting quietly and making your mind as still as possible. Ask your guide for protection then invite him to enter your aura. Get to recognise his presence. You might ask him to give you a sign that he is with you, such as a word or a sensation such as a touch on your hair. Allow yourself time to attune to his vibration, then listen for any words that come into your head. Repeat these words aloud, then wait for the next words and so on. You may begin in a very halting way but as you continue the words will come more quickly until, rather than listening then repeating, they will just flow without any conscious effort from you.

You will still be conscious while this is taking place but you will hear the words in a detached way, as if someone else was speaking them. How much you remember afterwards depends on the degree of trance. With practice, the trance will become progressively deeper. It may in time shade into a deep trance, at which point you will no longer be conscious and you will have no recollection afterwards of what was said through you.

Mediums who are developing this gift are often beset with self-doubts. They don't want to deceive themselves and others by claiming that everything they say is spirit-inspired when they are fully aware that some of the words and ideas emanate from their own minds. 'How can I get myself out of the way,' they want to know, 'so that it's spirit speaking and not me?'

Dwelling too much on this difficulty has an inhibiting effect and may prevent you from letting anything through at all! You have to recognise that overshadowing is a blending of minds. The guides will utilise your existing knowledge but they will build upon it. The best way you can help is to read and study as widely as possible in order to give them a wide range of knowledge to draw upon, but try to avoid forming fixed ideas or strong prejudices on any subject. The more closely you attune to your guides, the more strongly they will be able to impress your mind, until they will be able to impart information that goes beyond your knowledge.

One problem often experienced with inspired speaking is getting the first words out. Even if you can hear them in your mind, the very act of opening your mouth to speak breaks the delicate link. The best way to overcome this is to start things off yourself with a few words of introduction. It doesn't have to be anything profound – 'Good evening!' is always a promising beginning. 'Greetings!' will do if you must, but preferably not 'How!'. Then follow on with whatever comes into your mind. Once you have spoken a few sentences your guide will be able to take over more and more strongly, but if you don't start the ball rolling yourself in this way you will probably sit there in silence, getting more and more tense, and nothing will happen at all! Once you get used to linking with your guide in this way it will become easier.

You shouldn't necessarily expect your voice to change

very much. Guides, whatever their country of origin (and there is no reason why they should belong to an exotic race) are quite capable of mastering your language. They may speak with an accent, but this is mainly to identify themselves and distinguish their speech from the medium's. They may use gestures and mannerisms the medium wouldn't normally use, but it is still the medium's vocal cords that are being employed so, if you are a woman, don't imagine that a deep bass voice will suddenly issue from your mouth!

It's a good idea to have someone record your inspired speaking so that you can listen to it afterwards. This will enable you to judge the quality of what is coming through. There are a number of questions you should ask yourself. Does it contain material that is unknown to you or that you could not have expressed so well? No true guide will speak in a way that insults your dignity or intelligence. Most of all, is it given with love and perhaps a touch of kindly humour? If it is, you have a precious gift that should be cultivated.

No teaching or information that comes through in this way should be regarded as infallible. Apart from possible colouring from the medium's mind, which always has to be taken into consideration, guides and spirit teachers are still individuals with their own beliefs and opinions. They don't agree on every issue. But their knowledge is far greater than ours and, perhaps more importantly, they bring immense love from the higher dimensions which is poured into the medium and, through them, can touch the listeners' hearts.

From Inspired Speaking
To Deep Trance

Although some mediums do make the progression from inspired speaking to trance, some find it impossible to make that final step. There are a number of reasons for this. It may be that your guides do not think it necessary for you to work in this way. There may be some fear, at a subconscious level, holding back. Or it may be simply that you do not have the right conditions around you.

You need to sit in a circle of people with whom you are completely comfortable, led by a medium who has experience of trance work. There must be complete quiet. You will not be able to relax if you are afraid of being jolted back to reality by sudden noise such as the phone ringing. The room does not need to be in darkness but should be dimly lit.

The circle should be one that is dedicated to the development of trance. No clairvoyance should be allowed as this will waste the psychic energy. All the members of the group should agree that they are going to focus their attention on the person or persons who are attempting to go into trance. This needs commitment and unselfishness, and, human nature being what it is, it is not surprising that such circles are hard to find.

Trance should be approached in the same way as inspired speaking: asking for protection, inviting the guide to enter your aura, then starting things off by speaking the words that come to you. If, after a few months of trying this, in the conditions described, you still have no success, you should resign yourself to the fact that deep trance is not for you, or at least, that you are not yet ready for it. Your guides know what is best and you should trust their judgement.

Trance or inspired speaking is mainly for transmitting teaching from the spirit world, either in small groups or in spiritualist church services. I do not practice deep trance, but I frequently find myself being overshadowed while giving private sittings. This overshadowing tends not to come from the sitter's spirit loved ones, who are probably unable to tune into my mind sufficiently to permit them to communicate in this way. It usually comes from my guides or guides belonging to the sitter. I regard it as a very valuable form of mediumship because it enables me, to a large extent, to put my own mind aside, so the words of help or advice can be given. I am fully conscious, but the words seem to flow through me, rather than emanating from my mind and I know that the wisdom the guides bring goes beyond my own capability.

Growth In Channelling

After years of neglect, trance is now once again becoming popular. Another new phenomenon is also gaining in popularity. Channelling, which originated in America, is fast catching on over here. Though to the casual observer it resembles trance mediumship, the approach behind it is different in many ways.

Briefly, channelling can be defined as the art of bringing through teaching or information from other levels of consciousness. It is hard to be more precise. A channeller may be communicating with a deceased human being or a spirit guide. In this sense, all mediums are channellers. But while mediums have traditionally seen their role as attempting to prove life after death, channellers take a broader view. The source of the material they bring through may just as well be their own higher self.

How To Channel

Channelling appeals to those who are not necessarily concerned to contact spirit loved ones, but who wish to open their minds to the higher dimension in order to develop their spiritual awareness and knowledge. It is a skill most people can acquire. Try the following exercise.

▷ As with trance and inspired speaking, sit within your circle or with a person who is experienced in spirit communication. Say a prayer for protection. Focus your attention on the crown centre at the top of your head. Visualise it as a lotus unfolding. Imagine a light pouring down upon you from above your head, descending through all the chakras and filling every pore of your being.

Deepen your breathing. With every in-breath, draw in more light. With every out-breath expand your aura, reaching upwards into the spiritual universe. When you have reached as high as you can hold your mind steady and be receptive to whatever comes to you. It may be your guide who comes to speak through you, but it may be a higher part of your own being. Let the words flow without worrying about the source.

When you feel ready to come back, close down, using the same closing down exercise that should be used after any kind of psychic work.

Channelling can bring great benefits. As a way of linking with the higher dimension it is accessible to people who may not have the ability or inclination to work in the way of traditional mediumship. It does, however, have its dangers. In trance mediumship, the medium serves as the instrument for a particular guide who can be recognised and identified. As channelling is so much more open, it is easy for the subconscious mind to take over. You therefore need to be very discerning, both in assessing your own work and that of other channellers. Use your intuition and common sense to reject anything you are not comfortable with, or that does not ring true.

In channelling, as in all forms of mediumship, sincerity of intention is all-important. Like attracts like. Seek the light and you will become light. Give in love and you will receive love. The spirit world watches over our world with great tenderness and concern. There are many loving beings who are working to guide humankind forward into peace. It is the responsibility of everyone who is aware of the higher dimension to co-operate with them, to be instruments through which they can reach out to all who are in need, to teach and heal.

The other day, when I was taking a service at a small spiritualist church in Surrey, I glanced up during the singing of a hymn and saw the spirit form of my father sitting in the front row of seats. It was only a momentary glimpse, but it brought tears of emotion to my eyes. My thoughts went back to the day, over 20 years ago, when I attended his funeral. It was his death that had set me off on the long pathway of becoming a medium. And here he was, supporting and encouraging me as he had done when on earth, and as he had continued to do ever since he had entered that higher and more beautiful world.

I hope this book has helped you to realise that this continuing contact with those we love is available to us all. The spirit world is just a small step away. Build your own rainbow bridge to those you love. Go forward in love and light the way for others.

Useful Addresses

College of Psychic Studies, 16 Queensberry Place, London SW7 2EB. Lectures, seminars, workshops, courses on healing, mediumship and meditation, private consultations with sensitives.

Crystal Herbs, Waveney Lodge, Hoxne, Suffolk IP21 4AS. Suppliers of flower, gem and crystal essences.

Greater World Christian Spiritualist Association, 3–5 Conway Street, London W1P 5HA. Development and awareness groups, workshops, lectures, demonstrations of clairvoyance, services, healing, residential study groups and seminars in various venues outside London (see also page 179).

Institute of Spiritualist Mediums, Tara, Southend Arterial Road, Gidea Park, Romford, Essex RM2 6PL. Lectures and meetings in London and elsewhere for mediums, and all those interested in the subject. Help and advice given to development groups.

International Spiritualist Federation, c/o Redwoods, Stansted Hall, Stansted, Mountfitchet, Essex CM24 8UD. Promotes congresses to unite Spiritualists throughout the world.

The Lynwood Fellowship, Royes Ridge, Plough Hill, Caistor, Lincoln, LN7 6UR. Residential seminars in various locations with leading tutors, researchers and mediums.

The Noah's Ark Society for Physical Mediumship, Tree Tops, Hall Road, Cromer, Norfolk NR27 9JQ. Seminars, newsletters, advice given to circles attempting to develop this form of mediumship.

Rodney Peacock, 60 Downside Road, Sutton, Surrey SM2 5HP. Residential and non-residential seminars in various locations on spiritual development and other allied subjects.

PRISM (Psychical Research Involving Selected Mediums), 195 Greenbank Road, Darlington, Co. Durham DL3 6EY. Independent body researching into mediumship.

Psychic News, Clock Cottage, Stansted Hall, Stansted, Essex CM24 8UD. Weekly spiritualist newspaper.

Psychic Research Foundation, 210 Penn Road, Wolverhampton WV4 4AA. Training and self-development courses, field trips and special interest weekends.

Runnings Park, Croft Bank, West Malvern, Worcs WR14 4DU. Day and residential courses, and lectures on channelling, healing and self-development. School of Channelling and School of Healing.

Spiritualist Association of Great Britain, 33 Belgrave Square, London SW1X 8QB. Lectures, workshops, demonstrations of clairvoyance, healing, private sittings, courses in mediumship and healing.

Spiritualists National Union, The Arthur Findlay College, Stansted Hall, Stansted, Essex CM24 8UD. Residential courses on all aspects of mediumship, healing and allied subjects with leading tutors and mediums.

White Eagle Lodge, New Lands, Brewells Lane, Rake, Liss, Hampshire GU33 7HY and also at *9 St Mary Abbots Place, Kensington, London W8 6LS.* Religious services, meditation, healing, courses on related subjects. Residential courses and retreats at New Lands.

Overseas

American Federation of Spiritualist Churches Inc., 145 Herring Pond Road, Buzzards Bay, MA 02532, USA.

Centre of Spiritual Studies, PO Box 12234, Centrahil, 6006 Port Elizabeth, R. South Africa.

Greater World Christian Spiritualist Association, 3–5 Conway Street, London W1P 5HA, UK. The Association has affiliated churches throughout the UK, Northern Ireland, Channel Islands, Australia, Canada, Nigeria and South Africa.

National Spiritualists' Association Churches, c/o Rev. S. L. Snowman, PO Box 217, Lily Dale, New York 14752, USA.

Spiritualist Alliance (Auckland) Inc., PO Box 9477, 120 Carlton Gore Road, Newmarket, Auckland 1, New Zealand.

BIBLIOGRAPHY AND RECOMMENDED READING

Ian Currie, *You Cannot Die* (1995, Element Books)
Betty J. Eadie, *Embraced by the Light* (1994, Aquarian)
Oliver Fox, *Astral Projection* (1993, Citadel Press)
Alan Gauld, *Mediumship and Survival* (1982, Paladin)
Zoë Hagon, *Channelling* (1989, Prism Press)
Ronald Hearn, *The Little Dutch Boy* (1993, Book Guild)
Soozi Holbeche, *The Power of Your Dreams* (1992, Piatkus)
Elisabeth Kübler-Ross, *On Life After Death* (1991, Celestial Arts, California)
Richard Lazarus, *The Case Against Death* (1993, Warner Books)
Raymond Moody, *Life After Life* (1975, Bantam Books)
Dr Melvin Morse, *Transformed by the Light* (1993, Piatkus)
Sylvan Muldoon & Hereward Carrington, *The Projection of the Astral Body* (1968, Rider)
Robert Munroe, *Journeys Out of the Body* (1990, Souvenir Press)
F.W.H. Myers, *Human Personality and its Survival of Bodily Death* (1992, Pilgrim Books)
Tony Neate, *The Guide Book* (1986, Gateway Books)
Ivy Northage, *Mediumship Made Simple* (1986, Psychic Press)

Stephen O'Brien, *Angels by my Side* (1994, Bantam Books)

Stephen O'Brien, *A Gift of Golden Light* (1995, Bantam Books)

Karlis Osis, *Deathbed Observations by Physicians and Nurses* (1961, Parapsychology Foundation Inc., New York)

Joseph Ostrom, *Understanding Auras* (1993, Aquarian)

Naomi Ozaniec, *The Elements of the Chakras* (1991, Element Books)

Ursula Roberts, *All About Mediumship* (1994, Two Worlds)

D. Scott Rogo, *Life After Death* (1986, Aquarian)

Jane Sherwood, *The Country Beyond* (1969, The C.W. Daniel Co. Ltd)

Sir George Trevelyan, *Exploration Into God* (1991, Gateway Books)

Ruth White, *Working With Your Chakras* (1993, Piatkus)

Linda Williamson, *Mediums and Their Work* (1990, Robert Hale)

Linda Williamson, *Mediums and the Afterlife* (1992, Robert Hale)

INDEX